AIR CAMPAIGN

D-DAY 1944

The deadly failure of Allied heavy bombing on June 6

STEPHEN A. BOURQUE | ILLUSTRATED BY EDOUARD A. GROULT

OSPREY PUBLISHING
Bloomsbury Publishing Plc
Kemp House, Chawley Park, Cumnor Hill, Oxford OX2 9PH, UK
29 Earlsfort Terrace, Dublin 2, Ireland
1385 Broadway, 5th Floor, New York, NY 10018, USA
E-mail: info@ospreypublishing.com
www.ospreypublishing.com

OSPREY is a trademark of Osprey Publishing Ltd

First published in Great Britain in 2022

A catalog record for this book is available from the British Library.

ISBN: PB 9781472847232; eBook: 9781472847249;
ePDF: 9781472847218; XML: 9781472847225

22 23 24 25 26   10 9 8 7 6 5 4 3 2 1

Maps by bounford.com
Diagrams by Adam Tooby
3D BEVs by Paul Kime
Index by Zoe Ross
Typeset by PDQ Digital Media Solutions, Bungay, UK
Printed and bound in India by Replika Press Private Ltd.

To find out more about our authors and books visit www.ospreypublishing.com. Here
you will find extracts, author interviews, details of forthcoming events and the option to
sign up for our newsletter.

Acknowledgments
Writing during the COVID pandemic
has made this task far more complicated
than it should have been. However, I
was able to complete this work thanks
to the following: Steven Zaloga, the
master of detail who helped me start
this project and served as an inspiration
throughout; Elisabeth Dubuisson at the
Ike Skelton Combined Arms Reference
Library; Miranda Gilmore and Tammy
Horton (Air Force Historical Research
Agency) who I bothered many times and
who always cheerfully provided me with
the material I needed; Alex Bainbridge
(Penn State Special Collections Library)
who was especially helpful in getting
me in the door at this unique archive;
Mike Bechtold whose advice on all
things Canadian was beneficial; Richard
Drew whose Atlantikwall web page was
a solid reference on what was happening
and graciously sent me photographs
and details; Tim Nenninger (NARA
College Park), my long-time friend who
tolerated and abetted my many projects
for years; Andy Knapp, who has guided
me through the issues of bombing
French targets and understanding French
culture; André Rakoto, who has always
been available when confronted by
the peculiarities of the French archive
system; and Tom Milner at Osprey, who
has displayed a high degree of patience
and tolerance as he guided me through
this process. Thanks to all of you for
your support and assistance.
Special thanks also to Edouard Groult
who is an amazing artist and whose
efforts motivated me to work far
harder than I intended. Finally, my
wife, supporter and chief critic, Debra
Anderson, who has read every page of
this manuscript at least twice. Thanks for
your love and for catching most of my
mistakes in advance. However, any errors
that readers find are mine, and I beg
your tolerance and forgiveness.

CONTENTS

INTRODUCTION

Arthur Harris's favorite aircraft, the Avro Lancaster became Britain's standard heavy bomber, considered by most to be the best night bomber of the war. By the end of May 1944, Bomber Command had 852 Mark I and III aircraft assigned to its combat squadrons, especially Groups 1 and 5. With a crew of seven, it had eight machine guns and carried a normal bomb load of 12,000lb (5,443kg). An added advantage of this aircraft was it could be modified to carry extremely heavy bombs, such as the 12,000lb Tallboy designed for destroying large concrete structures, like V-2 launch sites and submarine pens. Overall, it could carry more pounds of bombs than any other aircraft in the Allied inventory. However, it was ineffective as a precision weapon in support of ground troops. (Daily Mirror/Mirrorpix/Mirrorpix via Getty Images)

Thirty minutes after midnight on June 6, 1944, 100 Lancaster and Halifax heavy bombers from Royal Air Force Bomber Command's No 1 Group approached the German artillery battery at Crisbecq on the Cotentin Peninsula. After dropping its 534 tons of bombs on the concrete emplacements and the nearby French villages below, the bomber group crossed the peninsula and then banked to the right to begin its short journey back to base in the United Kingdom. For more than six hours, heavy and medium bombers from the Allied air forces attacked hostile artillery batteries and defensive positions along five beaches that the Allied commanders had selected to land their soldiers on during the opening phase of Operation *Neptune*. By any measure, this coordinated assault was the most extensive bombing operation of World War II. When the last bombers departed before 0800hrs that morning, over 3,200 heavy and medium bombers from three air forces had dropped more than 10,275 (US) tons of bombs on the coast.

After this initial assault, Allied bombers would re-arm and conduct subsequent missions across France, striking bridges, road junctions, and transportation centers. In addition, fighters and fighter bombers attacked German troops throughout the day, preventing enemy torpedo boats from interfering with the assault, and provided air cover for the invasion force. Additionally, almost 2,000 transports carried airborne soldiers, gliders, and supplies to drop zones on both ends of the invasion zone. Some estimates suggest that more than 14,000 sorties took place over western France that morning.

It would seem, given the scale of this operation, that air commanders would laud this operation in the postwar accounts and official histories, as they had with lesser attacks on Hamburg, Berlin, Ploeşti, and Schweinfurt. Unfortunately, that has not been the case, and both the Royal Air Force and the US Air Force, especially in the decade after the war, sought to minimize accounts of this massive employment of heavy bombers. Two main reasons have contributed to the official downplaying of the event. The first has to do with the culture of the bomber commanders, none of whom wanted to participate in providing direct support to the ground forces that June morning. The role of the heavy bomber was, in their view, strategic. Neither Arthur Harris, commander of RAF Bomber Command, nor Carl A. Spaatz, commanding the

United States Strategic Air Forces, wanted to draw attention to their serving as General Dwight D. Eisenhower's long-range artillery. It was not part of their vision of strategic bombing, originating during the interwar years and developing as the *raison d'être* for both air force branches.

However, a more self-serving, almost sinister, reason to ignore operations that day centers on results: it was the least effective Allied air operation of the entire war. Unfortunately, except for the medium bomber attacks on Utah Beach, the aerial assault that morning was a dismal failure. The air bombardment of coastal batteries had little effect, and in several cases the German defenders carried on spirited exchanges with the invasion fleet's battleships and cruisers. Moreover, the US Eighth Air Force failed to neutralize any of its assigned targets that morning, resulting in enemy machine guns and artillery fire inflicting heavy casualties against the assault troops. Almost every book on the Normandy assault notes the ineffectiveness of the aerial bombardment and the first wave of assault troops paying the price for this failure. As historian Donald L. Miller pointed out: "There was no glory that day for the bomber boys. That morning, they had appeared suddenly and spectacularly over the enemy's coast defenses just before the first landing boats came ashore. Hampered by thick cloud cover and concerned about hitting their own troops, the lead bombers, using radar bombsight, delayed their releases. Five thousand tons of explosives fell harmlessly behind German coast positions." The bombardment killed few Germans, but more French civilians. It also permitted the enemy defenders to use all of their undamaged weapons in seeking to kill and repel the invading American, British, and Canadian forces without hindrance.

This book describes the details of this generally ignored operation. What was the plan? What should have happened? What actually occurred and why? What were the short-and long-term results? It also seeks to highlight the officers who planned and executed these operations. Unlike ground combat leaders, historians often do not give the air commanders the attention they deserve. Their decisions and conduct are a big part of why this operation did not achieve the standards requested by the ground commanders. This book also acknowledges the effect of the bombing operations on the French civilians who lived near the batteries and invasion beaches. Just like the German defenders and Allied airmen, they were participants in the dramatic events that June morning.

One of the most important fortifications on the Cotentin Peninsula, the Crisbecq Battery was the first installation the Allies attacked on June 6. The battery would remain operational throughout most of D-Day, and the Germans continued to defend it against American ground attacks until June 11. (US Army)

CHRONOLOGY

1944

16 January. Dwight D. Eisenhower arrives in England and assumes duties as Supreme Allied Commander.

21 March. Meeting of key players to discuss fire support in *Overlord* assault, involving all services and all major organizations. Present is Lt Gen Omar N. Bradley, commander of the US First Army that would land on Omaha and Utah beaches, and Lt Gen Miles Dempsey, in command of the British Second Army, that landed on Gold, Sword, and Juno beaches. The topic is the scope and intent of bombing missions against batteries and other coastal positions.

8 April. Publication of Joint Fire Plan.

14 May. Bradley submits changes to the Joint Fire Plan, asking the air component to attack specific fortifications and troop locations.

17 May. Dempsey submits final target list for Gold, Sword, and Juno beaches.

26 May. Second Allied Air Commander's Conference. Maj Gen James Doolittle, head of the Eighth US Air Force, reports his crews are proficient enough to hit a box 400 yards deep and 800 yards wide, as long as he has

General Dwight D. Eisenhower, the Supreme Allied Commander and responsible for Operation *Overlord* and its assault phase, Operation *Neptune*. His determination to use Bomber Command and the Eighth Air Force's bombers as his long range, flying artillery caused extreme angst among the air commanders. Taken on the afternoon of June 5, this photograph reflects Eisenhower's lack of direct involvement in planning and operations that day. (Photo12/Universal Images Group via Getty Images)

some natural terrain feature, such as a coastline or river, as a guide.

27 May. Eighth Air Force issues instructions to all air divisions to conduct experimental missions against three coastal batteries in the Pas de Calais area. Purpose of this mission is a test of H2X Pathfinder equipment to determine the feasibility of conducting overcast attacks against small targets and to gain proficiency in this type of operation. Subsequently on June 2, 3, 4, and 5, additional operations of this nature are carried out, and bombing is accomplished by releasing through overcast employing H2X methods. Fighter aircraft acting as spotters fly below overcast observing bombing results.

29 May. Analysis of results of camera bombing and bombing of French coast indicate good to excellent results might be expected when bombing beach areas through the overcast. The range error is slightly over, with only a few short strikes being observed.

3 June. Fifth Air Commander's Conference. Doolittle says that further experiments by Eighth Air Force in bombing beaches with H2X have been very successful.

4 June. All Pathfinder crews are briefed in the bombing techniques to be used. The importance of such an operation is stressed, with special emphasis on not releasing bombs in the Channel short of the invasion beaches. The crews are keyed up and eager to make all necessary preparations to ensure success, all crews feeling confident that the mission can be successfully accomplished in spite of overcast conditions.

5 June. Eighth Air Force planners second-guess original instructions. Within the headquarters, staff officers make the decision to change its coming plan, assuring the beach targets would not be neutralized as promised.

6 June. 0050hrs. Bomber Command commences attacks on artillery batteries.

0530hrs. Approximate beginning of naval bombardment.

0555hrs. Eighth Air Force 2nd Bombardment Division attacks targets on Omaha Beach.

0656hrs. Eighth Air Force 3rd Bombardment Division attacks targets on eastern Juno and Sword beaches.

0658hrs. Eighth Air Force 1st Bombardment Division attacks targets on Gold and western Juno beaches.

0600. Ninth Air Force attacks Utah Beach targets.

0630hrs. Landings begin. The air forces have neutralized only the German positions on Utah Beach. Casualties amongst landing troops and French civilians on other beaches high.

7 July. Gilger Commission report investigating bomb damage in Normandy.

8 Aug. "Parker Memorandum" acknowledges change of plan and states that Eisenhower and Leigh-Mallory, the Allied Expeditionary Air Forces commander, approved the change.

6 Nov. Eighth Air Force A-3 (Operations) publishes "Report of Operations-2–17 June 1944 Inclusive," incorporating details of Parker Memorandum.

1951

The United States Air Force publishes *The Army Air Forces in World War II. Europe: Argument to V-E Day, Volume Three: January 1944 to May 1945* (University of Chicago Press), incorporating the Parker Memorandum and alleging, without evidence, that Eisenhower had approved the change in bombing times. This remains the standard narrative of the aerial bombing effort.

The commander of the Allied Expeditionary Air Force, Air Marshal Trafford Leigh-Mallory. His peers and historians have never given him and his headquarters credit for their role in the invasion, even though they planned and coordinated the most massive use of air power in history. Determined to support the ground forces during the landing, Leigh-Mallory clashed with most senior air commanders, including Harris and Spaatz. He perished in an air crash in November 1944 and was unable to defend himself in the postwar flurry of commanders' memoirs. (Popperfoto via Getty Images)

Air Marshal Arthur W. Tedder, who previously served as commanding officer of RAF Middle East Command, was Eisenhower's choice to command the AEAF. Because of the conflict between Leigh-Mallory and other air commanders, he became the SHAEF deputy commander, coordinating air operations for Operation *Neptune* and bridging the divide between Leigh-Mallory and the bomber commanders. (SSPL/Getty Images)

ATTACKER'S CAPABILITIES

The Allied Expeditionary Air Force (AEAF)

No aspect of Operation *Neptune*, the landing phase of Operation *Overlord*, gave Dwight D. Eisenhower more headaches than its air command organization. Once President Franklin D. Roosevelt appointed him as the invasion commander in early December 1943, the new Supreme Commander, Allied Expeditionary Force, Eisenhower, assumed he would choose his deputy for air operations. Knowing that it needed to be a British officer, Eisenhower wanted Air Marshal Arthur Tedder to control all air operations before and during the invasion. However, Prime Minister Winston Churchill dashed such hopes by appointing Air Marshal Trafford Leigh-Mallory as the Allied Expeditionary Air Forces commander. The logic behind this appointment remains somewhat obscure, but it precipitated a constant stream of interpersonal conflict. Given the importance Eisenhower placed on unified air command, as he did for both the ground and naval portions of the assault, he was pretty angry at Leigh-Mallory assuming this critical position without any discussion.

Air Marshal Arthur T. Harris, commander of RAF Bomber Command, and General Carl A. Spaatz, commanding the US Strategic Air Forces, didn't have any intention of cooperating with Leigh-Mallory. Both were convinced that Operation *Overlord* was a waste of their precious heavy bombers, which they wanted to focus against German cities and factories. However, Eisenhower, Leigh-Mallory's boss, would accept nothing but control over all aviation in the European Theater of Operations during the invasion. Finally, after months of negotiations among the political authorities and military high command, the showdown came on March 25. Eisenhower made it clear that he intended to resign if the Combined Chiefs of Staff did not give him authority over Harris and Spaatz's forces in supporting the invasion.

The resignation was not required, as no one in the British government wanted Eisenhower to go; his replacement would have been Chief of Staff George C. Marshall, who was even less flexible on these matters. The outcome was that Leigh-Mallory commanded Arthur Coningham's RAF Second Tactical Air Force, RAF Coastal Command, Air Defense of

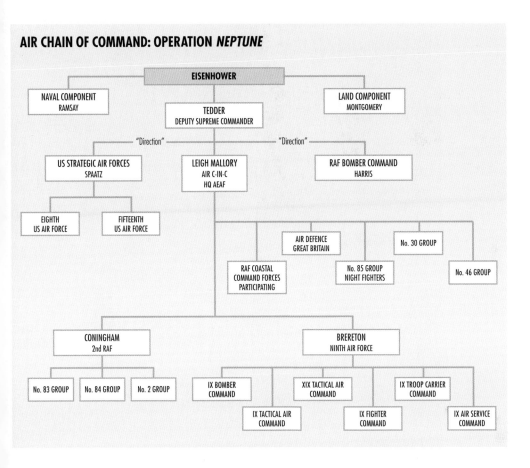

AIR CHAIN OF COMMAND: OPERATION *NEPTUNE*

```
                              EISENHOWER
         ┌───────────────────────┼───────────────────────┐
  NAVAL COMPONENT              TEDDER              LAND COMPONENT
      RAMSAY            DEPUTY SUPREME COMMANDER      MONTGOMERY

        "Direction"          │            "Direction"
  ┌──────────────────────────┼──────────────────────────┐
US STRATEGIC AIR FORCES   LEIGH MALLORY         RAF BOMBER COMMAND
      SPAATZ                AIR C-IN-C                 HARRIS
                            HQ AEAF
   ┌──────┴──────┐
 EIGHTH      FIFTEENTH
US AIR FORCE  US AIR FORCE

                          AIR DEFENCE
                         GREAT BRITAIN        No. 30 GROUP

                  RAF COASTAL          No. 85 GROUP
                  COMMAND FORCES       NIGHT FIGHTERS     No. 46 GROUP
                  PARTICIPATING

        CONINGHAM                           BRERETON
         2nd RAF                          NINTH AIR FORCE

 No. 83 GROUP  No. 84 GROUP  No. 2 GROUP   IX BOMBER      XIX TACTICAL AIR   IX TROOP CARRIER
                                           COMMAND        COMMAND            COMMAND
                                     IX TACTICAL AIR    IX FIGHTER      IX AIR SERVICE
                                     COMMAND            COMMAND         COMMAND
```

ABOVE ALLIED CHAIN OF COMMAND

Great Britain, several independent fighter groups, and Lewis Brereton's US Ninth Air Force. Tedder became Eisenhower's Deputy Supreme Commander, with a particular portfolio on coordinating air operations. As such, he not only supervised Leigh-Mallory but also "directed" Spaatz and Harris. In practice, when Tedder, General Bernard Montgomery (in charge of the ground assault), and Leigh-Mallory developed their operational plans and target lists, the bomber commanders had little choice but to comply or have a face-off with the Supreme Commander.

Capabilities of the air components

While the senior command structure could be somewhat dysfunctional, the four air forces and additional air units assigned to Operation *Neptune* represented the most potent air armada then ever assembled. While each possessed certain standard capabilities – air-to-air fighter support, for example – each brought unique skills to the landings air assault. The US Ninth and RAF Second Air Forces were tactical commands, equipped with medium bombers, fighter bombers, and fighters, to support the ground forces before, during, and after the invasion. They had the ability to precisely, by the standards of 1944, hit designated targets. In addition, both forces had impressive capabilities to neutralize enemy defensive installations, such as bunkers, gun positions, and trench lines, before the invading troops landed on the beach. These kinds of tactical air forces were an integral part of the armed forces of most belligerents during the war.

Lieutenant General Carl A. Spaatz, commander of US Strategic Air Forces in Europe. The overall US Air Force commander in the theater, he often clashed with Eisenhower and Leigh-Mallory over the use of his heavy bombers in support of Operation *Neptune*. He opposed using the Eighth Air Force on any bombing missions in France. (USAAF)

OPPOSITE
Photographed here in April 1944, Air Marshal Arthur T. Harris turned RAF Bomber Command into one of the most destructive military organizations in history. At its best when attacking German cities, it was an inappropriate tool for supporting troops during the invasion. (Leonard McCombe/ Picture Post/Hulton Archive/Getty Images)

Two other fighting organizations were unique to the United States and Great Britain. Based on the theories and writings of Giulio Douhet, William Mitchell, and Hugh Trenchard, advocates of strategic airpower believed the purpose of the bomber was to win wars by destroying the enemy's military and moral capability to wage it. The British Air Ministry and Headquarters, United States Army Air Force created RAF Bomber Command and the US Eighth Air Force with this purpose in mind. Both forces were equipped with hundreds of four-engine bombers capable of dispensing thousands of pounds of bombs deep into enemy territory. Additionally, the United States had the Fifteenth Air Force, which included four-engine bombers in the Mediterranean Theater of Operations. Lt Gen Carl A. Spaatz had operational control over both of these groups as commander, US Strategic Air Forces in Europe. However, during Operation *Neptune*, the heavy bombers would no longer operate in that strategic capability, working directly for the Combined Chiefs of Staff, but instead as tactical arms of Eisenhower's joint invasion force. Unfortunately, few air officers of either nation ever anticipated heavy bombers performing in that role.

AIRCRAFT AVAILABLE IN BOMBER COMMAND, EIGHTH AND NINTH AIR FORCES					
Aircraft name	Manufacturer	Type	Assigned to:	Max bomb load, lb (kg)	Aircraft available
A-20 Havoc	Douglas	Light Bomber	Ninth Air Force	2,600 (1,179)	150
B-26 Marauder	Martin	Medium Bomber	Ninth Air Force	3,000 (1,360)	392
Halifax	Handley-Page	Heavy Bomber	Bomber Command	13,000 (5,897)	521
Lancaster	Avro	Heavy Bomber	Bomber Command	12,000 (5,443)	852
B-17G Flying Fortress	Boeing	Heavy Bomber	Eighth Air Force	6,000 (2,721)	1,056
B-24 Liberator Bomber	Consolidated	Heavy Bomber	Eighth Air Force	8,800 (3,991)	912
Mosquito	de Havilland	Medium Bomber	Bomber Command	4,000 (1,810)	122
Stirling	Short Brothers	Heavy Bomber	Bomber Command	3,500 (1,600)	60

RAF Bomber Command

By the spring of 1944, Arthur Harris's Bomber Command was one of the world's two most potent air combat forces. With over 1,400 heavy bombers in 61 squadrons, it had become the nemesis of German cities, whose people had begun the war believing they were immune to modern bombardment from the air. Harris himself thought employing Bomber Command in support of Operation *Neptune* was a violation of the principles of strategic bombardment and a waste of his valuable aircraft. His most important weapon was the Avro Lancaster, with 852 assigned to flying squadrons. Most were Mark I and III versions.

Harris employed one additional aircraft, the de Havilland DH.98 Mosquito. A fast, versatile aircraft, it carried no defensive armament and depended on its speed for protection. Bomber Command had six squadrons (122 aircraft) configured as light bombers that carried up to 4,000lb (1,810kg) of ordnance. These were especially useful for precision raids. Harris had another four squadrons (68 aircraft) for bomber support. For standard bombing runs, the Mosquitoes served as pathfinder aircraft, carrying H2S radars, finding the target, and dropping flares to mark the targets for the following Lancaster and Halifax heavy bombers. (Roger Viollet via Getty Images)

Harris loved these aircraft and could never get enough of them. The command still had a few Stirlings remaining (43), but Harris had been replacing them since late 1942. The second most common aircraft was the Handley-Page Halifax III heavy bomber, with 521 assigned to combat groups. Harris also hated this aircraft and wanted it replaced as soon as possible. Both of these aircraft could carry huge bomb loads. Also flying for Bomber Command was the Mosquito light bomber. Probably the most versatile aircraft of the war, Harris had 122 performing different tasks across his command. Except for the Mosquito, none of these aircraft had any precision capability and little value in a ground support mission, as Harris argued in vain. In addition, Bomber Command executed most of its tasks during the night, adding to its overall inaccurate performance.

BOMBER COMMAND ORDER OF BATTLE: JUNE 1, 1944				
Group	Commander	# Aircraft	Type	Squadrons
No 1 Group	Edward A. B. Rice	200	Lancaster	11 squadrons, including 300 (Polish) and 460 (RAAF)
No 3 Group	Richard Harrison	117	Lancaster	6 Squadrons
		52	Stirling	2 Squadrons
		6	Halifax	Assigned to 161 Squadron
		10	Lysander	Assigned to 161 Squadron
		6	Hudson	Assigned to 161 Squadron

No 4 Group	Charles Roderick Carr	208	Halifax	11 Squadrons, including 346 (Free French) and 466 (RAAF)
No 5 Group	Ralph A. Cochrane	240	Lancaster	15 Squadrons, including two Pathfinder (463–467), 44 (Rhodesia), 463 and 467 RAAF
		16	Mosquito	627 Squadron (Pathfinder)
No 6 Group (RCAF)	Clifford M. McEwen	160	Halifax	10 Squadrons
		48	Lancaster	3 Squadrons
No 8 Group (Pathfinder)	Don Bennett	96	Lancaster	7 Squadrons
		80	Mosquito	5 Squadrons
	Total Aircraft in Squadrons	1,239		

RAF Second Tactical Air Force and other British commands

Air Marshal Arthur Coningham's Second Tactical Air Force, Air Marshal Roderic Hill's Air Defense of Great Britain (formally Fighter Command), and Air Chief Marshal Sholto Douglas's Coastal Command did not participate in the bombing of the Normandy beaches on June 6. Cumulatively, these forces operated over 3,600 fighters, fighter bombers, medium bombers, and various heavy bombers. Their role in Operation *Neptune* was to protect the skies over invasion routes and the beachhead, deny German naval and air interdiction of the invasion force, and attack German troops and installations beyond the invasion zone. These commands had eighteen squadrons of Typhoon fighter bombers,

Air Marshal Arthur Coningham's 2nd Tactical Air Force did not participate in the bombing of the Normandy beaches on June 6. Given the inaccuracy of the Eighth Air Force, perhaps planners should have assigned it some of the important missions on the beaches. Coningham is here photographed on the left, with MajGen Brereton. (Hulton Archive/Getty Images)

four squadrons of Mitchell B-25 medium bombers, and two squadrons of Boston light bombers. AEAF planners employed these against targets beyond the landing zone during the first mission on June 6. However, given the Eighth Air Force's ineffectiveness in supporting the landings, the decision not to employ some of Coningham's most effective aircraft against German defenses on Gold, Sword, and Juno beaches was probably a mistake.

US Ninth Air Force

Major General Louis Brereton's Ninth Air Force was the American contribution to the AEAF organization, with over 2,700 aircraft of all kinds (except for heavy bombers). It was a tactical organization designed to support ground forces and deploy behind the advancing US Army once the beachhead was secure. For the D-Day assault, Maj Gen Samuel Anderson's IX Bomber Command was the principal attacking force. Organized into three wings (97th, 98th, and 99th), the A-20 Havoc light bomber and the B-26 Marauder medium bomber were its weapons. These excellent platforms allowed crews to fly at relatively low level and hit their targets with a high degree of accuracy.

NINTH AIR FORCE, IX BOMBER COMMAND				
Wing	Commander	Groups	Aircraft	Type
97th Combat Wing	Chris H. W. Rueter	409, 410, 416	288	A-20 Light Bombers
98th Combat Wing	Millard Lewis	323, 387, 394, 397	384	B-26 Medium Bombers
99th Combat Wing	Charles F. Salter	322, 344, 386, 391	384	B-26 Medium Bombers
Total aircraft assigned to groups			1,056	

US Eighth Air Force

Major General James H. Doolittle was already an American hero before taking command of the US Eighth Air Force in January 1944. His carrier-based raid with B-25 Mitchell medium bombers against Japan had been one of the few American achievements during the first six months of the war. By June 1, 1944, his Eighth Air Force had 1,056 B-17 – primarily the G-Model, Flying Fortress – and 912 Consolidated B-24 Liberator bombers at his disposal. However, as in the case of Bomber Command, the nature of these heavy aircraft, akin to using a sledgehammer to hit a small nail, limited their ability to affect the battle as the ground generals desired. Doolittle's command consisted of three bombardment divisions, each with four combat wings.

US EIGHTH AIR FORCE					
Division	Wing	Commander	Groups	Aircraft	Type
1st Bomb Div		Robert Williams		450	
	1st	William M. Gross	91, 381, 398		B-17
	40th	Howard M. Turner	92, 305, 306		B-17
	41st	Robert F. Travis	303, 379, 384		B-17
	94th	Julius K. Lacey	351, 401, 457		B-17
2nd Bomb Div		James P. Hodges		450	
	2nd	Edward J. Timberlake Jr	389, 445, 453		B-24
	14th	Leon W. Johnson	44, 392, 492		B-24
	20th	Jack W. Wood	93, 446, 448		B-24
	95th	Frederick R. Dent, Jr	489, 491		B-24
	96th	James H. Isbell	458, 466, 467		B-24
3rd Bomb Div		Curtis E. LeMay		354	B-17
				96	B-24
	4th	Frederick W. Castle	94, 385, 447,		B-17
	13th	Edgar M. Wittan	95, 100, 390		B-17
	45th	Archie J. Old, Jr.	96, 388, 452		B-17
	92nd	Harold Q. Huglin	486, 487		B-24
	93rd	Walter R. Peck	34, 490, 493		B-24
Total Aircraft Employed, 1st Mission, June 6				1,350	

Ordnance

Most of the bombs used during the assault were general-purpose (GP or MC) bombs. Depending on the fuze, those that explode above the ground cause destruction by blast and vacuum pressure, while those that hit the ground cause damage from the shock of the explosion. Both are essentially the same, differing by size, overall weight, and weight of the explosives. For its first mission on D-Day, the Eighth Air Force used 100lb, 500lb, and 1,000lb bombs of this type. It also employed fragmentation (FRAG) bombs. Upon explosion, before hitting the ground, these munitions shattered into many metal fragments that ripped into exposed troops and light equipment. These were small bombs, weighing only 20lb. For delivery, ground crews assembled them in clusters of 100–120lb each. Bomber Command utilized 500lb and 1,000lb Medium Capacity bombs, essentially general-purpose, for its D-Day missions.

Assorted ordnance for the 398th Bomb Group ready to load. Most B-17 loads on June 6 were 100lb or 500lb bombs. (USAAF, Eberly Family Special Collections Library, Penn State University Libraries)

Depending on the target, squadron support crews fixed each bomb with the appropriate fuze, a mechanical device that sets off a bomb at the desired time. Ground crews could set them to explode at various heights in the air, upon impact with the ground, or after a delay.

ALLIED AIR FORCES' BOMB TYPES USED ON D-DAY			
Type	Weight (lb)	Air Force	Comment
AN-M30 GP	100	Eighth AF	General Purpose
AN-M41 FRAG	20	Eighth AF	Fragmentation bomb. Fitted into 100lb delivery clusters
AN-M57 GP	250	Ninth AF	General Purpose
MC	500	Bomber Command	General Purpose
AN-M64 GP	500	Eighth AF	General Purpose
MC	1,000	Bomber Command	General Purpose
AN-M65 GP	1,000	Eighth AF	General Purpose

Navigation and targeting

The first problem for attacking formations was to find the assigned target area. Although navigation technology had improved by early 1944, locating the correct city, rail yard, or factory was still challenging. Finding a small cluster of bunkers along a beach or camouflaged artillery behind the coast was even more challenging. Before World War II, the standard method of air navigation was by visual observation – essentially using maps to fly from landmark to landmark – or radio direction, following radio signals from one town to the next. In some cases, navigators could also use astronavigation, just like ancient mariners. These methods are not feasible during wartime, as the enemy can shoot down aircraft flying too low and slow, and interfere with radio broadcast signals. Furthermore, once near the target, smoke, bad weather, and enemy antiaircraft fire make identifying specific locations or structures difficult. In the early stages of the war, air units had much trouble finding their targets and regularly flew to the wrong place. Therefore, scientists in both the British Commonwealth and the United States devoted much effort to developing and improving devices to overcome these challenges.

Unfortunately, in 1944, it was still almost impossible for heavy bombers to target their objectives with any degree of accuracy. Once aircraft arrived in the target area, the bombardier had to identify the assigned target on the ground, a difficult task in itself. Then the plane needed to drop its load of bombs at the right time to hit the enemy position. At the target, the aircraft would be flying at 130–150mph and bombing at altitudes of between 14,000 and 18,000ft. It was a complex challenge for the bombardier to determine precisely when to release the bombs. Air pressure, temperature, wind, turbulence, aircraft attitude, and enemy antiaircraft fire all magnified the problem of identifying release times. Heavy cloud cover made all of these computations more difficult. For the *Neptune* assault, finding the general area of attack was not that difficult, since all of these bombing objectives were relatively close to England. Getting to the general target area would not be a problem; hitting what the army asked for would be.

Oboe

This early navigation system consisted of two radio stations transmitting pulses. The Oboe-equipped aircraft detected these emissions and bounced them back to the stations. These

A B-17G Flying Fortress, the most famous American heavy bomber of the war. The aircraft was developed in the 1930s and constantly modified and improved by the US Army Air Force until it was replaced by the B-29 Superfortress, especially in the Pacific. It had a crew of ten, 12 machine guns, and could deliver 4,000–7,000lb of bombs. (USAAF, Eberly Family Special Collections Library, Penn State University Libraries)

While the B-17 is more famous, the B-24 Liberator was the workhorse of the strategic air forces for most of the war in the Mediterranean and Europe. The D-model had a crew of ten, ten .50cal machine guns and carried 5,000–8,000lb of bombs. As with all heavy bombers, it had little precision capability, and was not suited for small targets. (USAAF, Eberly Family Special Collections Library, Penn State University Libraries)

returns were measured and permitted the ground stations to determine the aircraft's distance from the station. The two ground stations then worked together to coordinate the aircraft's final approach over the target and when to drop its bombs. It was more accurate than later systems and could help bombers find their way within a few hundred yards of the target. The system's major limitation was that it could only work with one aircraft at a time, so only the lead aircraft had an Oboe device, with others dropping their bombs on cue. Another limitation was that it only worked by line-of-sight and within 270 miles of the radio stations. It was also easy for the Germans to jam and intercept the transmissions. By 1944, neither Allied air force used this device extensively, although Bomber Command's No 6 Group of Pathfinders employed it for the first raids that morning.

GEE (TR 1335)

One of the first systems used by Bomber Command, and later the US Army Air Force, was GEE (TR 1335), which used radio signals from known transmitters. A master station emitted a pulse signal, while simultaneously, two secondary stations a distance away – called slave stations – also broadcast signals. An aircraft's onboard GEE system received these signals and portrayed them on a screen as lines called GEE coordinates. The navigator compared these coordinate lines to information on a map. The resulting computations gave the aircraft commander a reasonably accurate assessment of his location and the direction and time to his assigned target. However, the system required a line-of-sight back to the transmitter. Its usefulness, therefore, was limited to under 350 miles. Furthermore, its accuracy was inadequate for precise bombing missions, and ranged from ½ a mile to almost five miles from the target. There was also a constant technological struggle as German scientists sought to interfere with these transmissions, so it was always under technical improvement. Thus, while Bomber Command was comfortable using this device to determine when to drop bombs on a target, it was far too inaccurate and limited for American purposes.

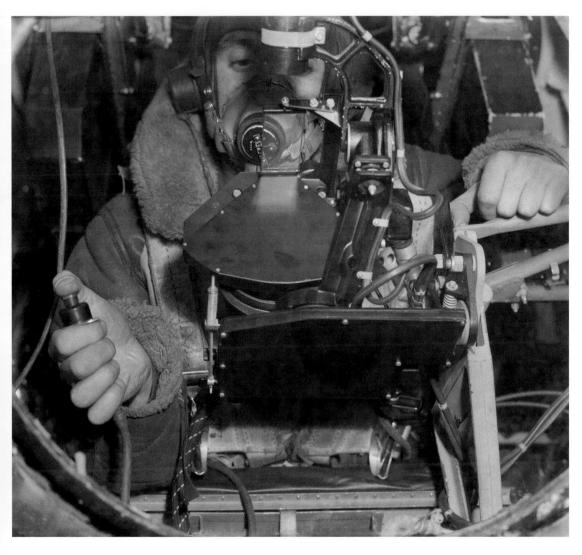

Mark XIV bombsight

Bomber Command used the Mark XIV bombsight. Like all such systems, it attempted to improve the bombardier's ability to deliver his munitions on the target. The Mark XIV was not a precision device, but Harris was content with an average error of more than 300 yards from the objective. It worked much better on bombing ranges, but the reality of operating in a combat environment seriously degraded its effectiveness. However, since Bomber Command, generally, was not seeking precision strikes at night, it was good enough for its purposes.

Norden bombsight

Once in the target area, in contrast to British area bombing practices, the US Army Air Force was determined, from the beginning, to conduct precision bombing, with minor collateral damage to civilians in the target area. The problem was that so many factors influenced bombing accuracy. Standard factors included wind speed near the target, air pressure, and the aircraft's speed, altitude, and attitude. The US Air Force's solution to these issues was the Norden bombsight. A costly, complicated, and secret device, it was supposed to solve these complex tasks. Unfortunately, while it may have worked well during individual trials in the western United States, its ability to contribute to accurate bombing runs during the D-Day

Bombardier using a British Mark XIV bombsight in a Lancaster in 1944. Referred to as the "area sight," it helped stabilize the aircraft when dropping its ordnance. It was not a precision system and was ineffective against small targets, such as coastal batteries. (IWM CH 12283)

The Norden bombsight. While it may have worked well during individual trials in the western United States, its ability to contribute to accurate bombing runs during the D-Day operation was marginal, especially given the nature of the targets and the overcast conditions that morning. (DoD)

operation was marginal, for several fundamental reasons. Firstly, clouds in northwest Europe generally obscured the ground below, not allowing the lead aircraft bombardier to identify the target positively. Secondly, they flew in formations of six or more aircraft, which all dropped their bombs on the cue of the lead bomber. In addition, the combat environment, German antiaircraft fire, enemy fighters, crew cabin temperature, proficiency, and fatigue all

Operator's station for H2X ground-scanning radar. A primitive system, it was the only means by which the navigator could identify the target area on the morning of June 6. (USAAF)

contributed to bombing inaccuracy. And no matter how accurate the first bombardier was, the others – up to 36 aircraft in the formation – dropped their loads after the lead aircraft. As a result, bombs could land almost anywhere within ½ a mile or more from the objective. By the end of May 1944, the Eighth Air Force reported that only 37 percent of all bombs dropped landed within 1,000 feet of the intended target. The Norden bombsight was better than nothing – but over Normandy that day in June, not by much.

H2X/H2S navigation radar

By 1944, the H2X radar (formally the AN/APS-15 Ground Scanning System) was the principal navigation device used by the Eighth Air Force. This radar was an American modification of the British H2S radar, the first ground mapping radar used in combat. The first H2X-equipped B-17s arrived in England in early February 1944, and Doolittle's command used it on its first mission later that month. Aircraft with these systems were called Pathfinders and, generally, only one aircraft in a dozen had this device. On these bombers, technicians removed the underside ball turret machine guns and inserted the H2X's rotating dish antenna. In the B-17, the internal controls, called "Mickey set," were installed in the radio room just behind the bomb bay. For B-24s, the system was on the flight deck behind the co-pilot.

Approaching the target area, the Mickey operator told the pilot what headings to take. Then, at the beginning of the bomb run, he coordinated his observations with the bombardier. However, the system's primary purpose was navigation during daylight overcast conditions and nighttime operations, not a targeting radar. The operator could only see a primitive map on an oscilloscope. It had no capability of distinguishing features on the ground, such as factories

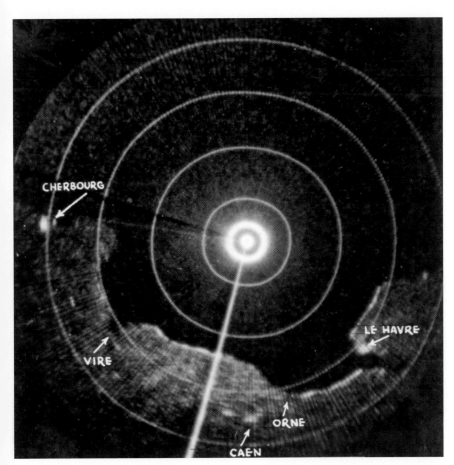

This airborne H2X radar scope image of the Normandy coastline was taken just before the invasion. The area would never look the same again during the war as it would be filled with military shipping. Doolittle was confident his navigators could use this scope to arrive over their assigned targets that morning. (USAAF)

LEFT EIGHTH AND NINTH AIR FORCES D-DAY FORMATION

Heavy bombers flew in combat formations, and never alone. RAF Bomber Command's method was to "stream" as many aircraft as possible over a single location in the shortest period of time. This method's intent, developed as a result of its night bombing experience, was to overload the German defenses. The Eighth Air Force built its formations on a three-aircraft "Vee" formation, one aircraft forward and two trailing on each side. The width of each of these groups was 390ft. Trailing bombers released their loads on visual cue from the lead aircraft, with no attempt to aim their bombs at a target. On June 6, planners based all missions on squadrons of six aircraft each. The Ninth Air Force also used the "Vee" formation but, because they flew low enough to see the targets, aircraft commanders had some flexibility as to how they attacked each target.

390ft

or rail marshaling yards. Once the operator believed he was over the target, he dropped his marker flares, and the other aircraft began dropping their bombs. It was an incredibly inaccurate operation, and most crews referred to it as "blind bombing." Unfortunately, this term did not sit well with General Henry ("Hap") Arnold and his US Army Air Force leaders, so generally, they referred to it in reports as "overcast bombing technique."

Few aircraft in June 1944 had this equipment, so it depended on the lead, Pathfinder radar operator. Once he identified the target through his scope, he told the bombardier to drop his illuminated markers. Then the other 17 or more bombardiers, flying in their large box formation, did the same. The result was a vast pattern that hit the assigned target only by chance. Neither Spaatz nor Doolittle had any faith in the H2X system, although it continued to improve unit performance. While the system helped guide aircraft to their targets, it was not designed or effective as a targeting radar.

However General Doolittle was one of the most persistent officers in the US Air Force and wanted to do everything he could to accomplish his assigned task. So on May 26, less than two weeks before the anticipated landings on June 5, the key aviation commanders met at AEAF headquarters. Doolittle reported that his command had been practicing bombing with H2X along the coast 100 miles north of the *Neptune* landing zone, using four groups of 18 bombers to determine how effective his force could be in hitting coastal targets. In his tests, the average error in range was 400 yards and the average deflection 800 yards. From these trials, he deduced that, excluding gross error, the Eighth Air Force could bomb within an accuracy of ½ a mile provided there were certain definite physical features such as a coastline and a river to guide them. If army leaders would accept a bombing accuracy of ½ a mile from the target, and if the weather conditions allowed for his bombers to take off, "he was prepared to undertake any task allotted to the Eighth Air Force." He also noted that he was grounding all H2X aircraft for two days before D-Day to ensure that every plane equipped with this aid would be available to operate when the time came. Doolittle's confidence must have been reassuring to Leigh-Mallory and Tedder, who had to coordinate air operations with the ground commanders.

DEFENDER'S CAPABILITIES

Fortifications on the French coast

Overview

With the possible exception of the Gettysburg battlefield in Pennsylvania, no stretch of defensive terrain has received more attention from historians than the beach area from Saint-Martin-de-Varreville on the Cotentin Peninsula to Merville, east of Ouistreham. Along this 65-mile stretch of coast, the Wehrmacht scattered small units from two stationary infantry divisions (the 716th and 709th) and one standard infantry division (the 352nd) in more than 45 fighting positions, called *Widerstandsnest* (resistance nests). Located at critical locations on or behind these defenses were 31 artillery installations to support the forward defenses by indirect fire against landing troops or direct fire against naval vessels. While all of these installations offered soldiers and equipment some protection from air bombardment, that was a secondary purpose. Responding to the massive bombing operation the Allies were planning was not a primary focus of the defensive planners. Additionally, the Luftwaffe had fewer than 200 aircraft stationed in the area. Consequently, the primary purpose of the artillery was not protecting installations from bombers but the destruction of Allied landing forces in the invasion zone. Therefore, the ground troops were on their own, and German defensive capabilities centered on passive and active air defense measures.

R677 bunker at WN72, Vierville-sur-Mer. With walls of steel-reinforced concrete 6½ft (2 meters) thick, this formidable strongpoint was well protected from artillery fire and the standard bombs dispensed by Allied bombers. Those inside survived the bombardment and engaged the US 116th Infantry Regiment when it arrived on Omaha Beach. The army used the balloon on top to deter German air attack early in the landing. (Galerie Bilderwelt/Getty Images)

GERMAN ORDER OF BATTLE, JUNE 1944				
Unit	Commander	Headquarters	Sector	Strength
709th Inf Div	Karl-William von Schlieben	Château de Chiffrevast (Valognes)	Utah	12,320
Grenadier Regt 729 (F)*	Helmuth Rohrbach	Le Vicel		
Grenadier Regt 739 (F)	Walter Köhn	Querqueville		
Grenadier Regt 919	Günther Keil	Montebourg		
Artillery Regt 1709	Robert Reiter	Equerdreville		

716th Inf Div	William Richter	La Folie-Couvrechet (Caen)	Gold/ Juno/ Sword	7,771
Grenadier Regt 726	Walter Korfes	Château de Sully		
Grenadier Regt 736	Ludwig Krug	Colleville-sur-Orne		
Fast-Brigade 30	Hugo Freiherr von Aufsess	Coutances		
Heavy Artillery Bn 989	Unk	Reviers		
Artillery Regt 1716	Helmut Knüpe	La Folie-Couvrechef (Caen)		
352nd Inf Div	Dietrich Kraiss	Littry	Omaha	12,734
Grenadier Regt 914	Ernst Heyna	Neuilly-la-Forêt		
Grenadier Regt 915	Karl Meyer	St-Paul-du-Vernay		
Grenadier Regt 916	Ernst Goth	Trévières		
Artillery Regt 352	Kurt-William Ocker	Tourteville		
Panzerjäger Bn 352	Werner Jahn	Vouilly		
Flaksturmregiment 1	Werner von Kistowski	Bayeux	Utah	4,216
Coast Artillery Regiment 1261	Gerhard Tripei	Le Poteau	Utah	

* (F) = Festung (Fortress/static)

Passive air defense

Given the short time between detection of Allied aircraft and their dropping bombs, German defenders had little opportunity to take cover in their predesignated air-raid shelters. All of these locations were in or very close to the actual fighting positions. The defenders intended to withstand the bombardment and then return to the fighting position to confront the landing force. The Germans had an extensive array of concrete structures designed to withstand naval and air bombardment. Examples include the concrete R677 bunker at WN72, Vierville-sur-Mer. With walls of steel-reinforced concrete 6½ft (2 meters) thick, this formidable strongpoint, housing an 88mm gun sited to sweep what the Allies called Omaha Beach, was generally protected from artillery fire and the standard bombs dispensed by tactical air forces.

Another example of defenders protected from air bombardment were those operating the naval artillery batteries, such as WN48, the battery on the edge of Gold and Omaha beaches at Longues-sur-Mer. Each M 272 gun Casemate had over 6½ft (2 meters) of concrete on all

The German defenders dug these prefabricated "Tobruk" concrete fighting positions into the ground to boost a strongpoint's overall defense. The concrete and earth on top protected crews from most bombardment effects. (Richard Drew, Atlantikwall.com)

sides and its ceiling, protecting each of its 150mm naval guns. Scattered nearby were other shelters for soldiers and ammunition, dug in and with reinforced overhead cover.

Finally, the third kind of defensive position was the "Tobruk." The German defenders dug these prefabricated concrete fighting positions into the ground as a strongpoint's overall defense. From the ring stand portion of the structure, the defenders could mount machine guns, small antitank guns, mortars, and even the turrets of obsolete French tanks. Within each position was a small, covered space for ammunition and to provide crews protection from air assault. Egress was from a small door that, generally, connected to a trench line.

Most of the soldiers manning defensive positions in Normandy had no overhead cover. These included those manning trenches, exposed guns on ring stands, and field artillery batteries positioned behind the front lines. Within a few feet of these positions were bunkers for ammunition and crew accommodations and protection, such as the six-man shelter that is prominent on Utah Beach. These positions were, where possible, dug into the ground, camouflaged, and protected from direct observation. Roofing could protect from near misses and stray bombs, but not a direct hit from 100–500lb bombs. Once they had the signal that aircraft were approaching, crews ran for cover to their designated shelter and waited for the call to emerge and return to their battle stations.

Active air defense

By June 1944, Germany had a well-developed antiaircraft establishment. Called Flak, for *Fliegerabwehrkanone* (literally "aviator-defense gun") units, they had an impressive array of weapons. Light Flak guns consisted of 20mm, 37mm, and 40mm guns. These could be mounted as single guns, in pairs, or on a four-gun mount. All but the 20mm could hit Eighth Air Force and Bomber Command aircraft during their attack runs. The most famous and familiar heavy air defense weapon was the 88mm gun, which could hit targets at 35,000ft. It was a double-threat weapon because it was also the world's best antitank gun.

Able to engage targets up to 33,000ft, the German 88mm antiaircraft gun was the most dangerous threat to Allied bombers. Twenty-four of these mobile guns were near Omaha Beach. Some of these had the chance to engage Allied bombers, shooting down several that morning. (Getty Images)

General Wolfgang Pickert, commanding the III Flakkorps, supervised mobile air defense operations between the River Somme and Normandy. Only one of his four regiments, Colonel Werner von Kistowski's Flaksturmregiment 1, was in the invasion area. This was a fully motorized regiment with three artillery battalions: the 497th and 226th were mixed units, each with 12 88mm guns (8.8cm Flak 37), 30 single-barrel 20mm guns (2.0cm Flak 38), and 18 four-barrel 20mm guns (2.0cm Flakvierling 38); the 90th Battalion was a light unit, with 27 2.0cm Flak 38s and nine Flakvierling 38s. Its authorized strength was 4,216 soldiers. On June 5, the regiment arrived in the Normandy area and established a temporary bivouac at La Cambe. In accordance with air defense doctrine, most units positioned themselves behind the lines between Isigny and Bayeux.

Few of the fighting positions on the coast had any air defense capability, with the possible exception of the machine guns at extremely close range. More dangerous for attacking aircraft were the air defense batteries integrated into the defenses of the coastal artillery batteries and the radar station at Douvres-la-Délivrande. These three-gun batteries, primarily 20mm and 37mm guns, had the task of close-in air defense against fighter bombers. Most fortifications had one battery, but some, such as Crisbecq, had two. They could also be sited to support the ground defenses. Almost all occupied ring stands in the open or on top of an artillery casemate. None of them were capable of inflicting much harm to the heavy bombers flying at 14,000ft.

CAMPAIGN OBJECTIVES
The vital beachhead

The 97th Bomb Wing (Light) had 193 A-20G light bombers. With a crew of three, it could carry 4,000lb of bombs. Its other major armament was a nose cone containing four 20mm Hispano cannons, and two M-2 Browning .50cal machine guns, making it an excellent aircraft for attacking enemy defensive positions. Note that this squadron is flying in its standard formation. (Roger Viollet via Getty Images)

Operation *Overlord* was the overall code name for the Allied invasion of Northwest Europe. Because of its scale, the original invasion planners, COSSAC (Chief of Staff to Supreme Allied Commander), organized their plans into several separate named operations. The most important of these was *Neptune*, the operation's assault phase. It generally encompassed all events from the departure from ports on June 4 until the invading forces had secured the lodgment, by approximately June 30, with the American seizure of Cherbourg. *Neptune* was a joint operation, the coordinated employment of army, navy, and air force units directed by a single commander. It was also a combined operation, in which forces from multiple nations fought toward a common objective under a single commander. By any measure, this was the most extensive and most complicated Allied endeavor of the entire war.

As mentioned earlier, General Eisenhower became Supreme Commander and Air Chief Marshal Tedder was his deputy. Each of the combined services had its unique commander and staff to control its operational domain. British flag officers became the commanders of the combined service commands: Admiral Bertram Ramsay for naval forces, Air Chief Marshal Trafford Leigh-Mallory for the air forces, and General Bernard Montgomery for the ground assault. Montgomery's principal subordinates, who would command the ground forces, were Lt Gen Omar Bradley for the US First Army and Lt Gen Miles Dempsey for the British Second Army. Building on their experience in the Mediterranean Theater of Operations, this structure generally worked well for the Allies, certainly better than any other similar organization up to that point in history.

The Joint Fire Plan

From January – when Eisenhower assumed control of the COSSAC planning effort – until April, representatives from all three components developed a general outline for coordinating supporting fire during the assault. Target selection depended upon what the naval forces needed

Responsible for Operation *Dynamo*, the British evacuation at Dunkirk in 1940, Admiral Bertram Ramsay returned to France as the commander of the Allied Naval Expeditionary Force. His fleet, especially the transports, depended on bombers neutralizing German batteries. In the end, it was his fighting ships which neutralized most of the heavy coastal guns. (Keystone/Hulton Archive/Getty Images)

to deliver the soldiers to the beach, and then what the army and corps commanders wanted to facilitate seizing their beach objectives. The Joint Fire Plan, published on April 8 and signed by the chiefs of staff of each of the component commanders, provided the guidelines for air and naval gunfire support during the invasion. The staff of Montgomery's 21st Army Group (comprising the US First Army and British Second Army) took the lead in identifying the enemy positions they wanted destroyed or neutralized, while Ramsay and Leigh-Mallory's planners determined the facilities or installations they needed to attack to support the landing. The first group of targets was the artillery batteries – such as those at Mereville, Longues-sur-Mer, and Crisbecq – that could interfere with the approaching invasion fleet. Therefore, Bomber Command was to attack them first, beginning just after midnight. The plan next focused on attacking the prepared German positions: "The importance of neutralizing the beach defenses

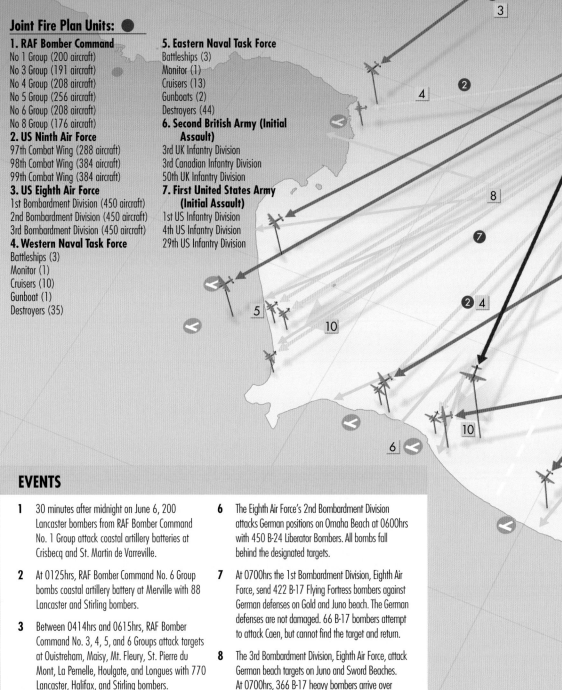

Joint Fire Plan Units: ●

1. RAF Bomber Command
No 1 Group (200 aircraft)
No 3 Group (191 aircraft)
No 4 Group (208 aircraft)
No 5 Group (256 aircraft)
No 6 Group (208 aircraft)
No 8 Group (176 aircraft)

2. US Ninth Air Force
97th Combat Wing (288 aircraft)
98th Combat Wing (384 aircraft)
99th Combat Wing (384 aircraft)

3. US Eighth Air Force
1st Bombardment Division (450 aircraft)
2nd Bombardment Division (450 aircraft)
3rd Bombardment Division (450 aircraft)

4. Western Naval Task Force
Battleships (3)
Monitor (1)
Cruisers (10)
Gunboat (1)
Destroyers (35)

5. Eastern Naval Task Force
Battleships (3)
Monitor (1)
Cruisers (13)
Gunboats (2)
Destroyers (44)

6. Second British Army (Initial Assault)
3rd UK Infantry Division
3rd Canadian Infantry Division
50th UK Infantry Division

7. First United States Army (Initial Assault)
1st US Infantry Division
4th US Infantry Division
29th US Infantry Division

EVENTS

1 30 minutes after midnight on June 6, 200 Lancaster bombers from RAF Bomber Command No. 1 Group attack coastal artillery batteries at Crisbecq and St. Martin de Varreville.

2 At 0125hrs, RAF Bomber Command No. 6 Group bombs coastal artillery battery at Merville with 88 Lancaster and Stirling bombers.

3 Between 0414hrs and 0615hrs, RAF Bomber Command No. 3, 4, 5, and 6 Groups attack targets at Ouistreham, Maisy, Mt. Fleury, St. Pierre du Mont, La Pernelle, Houlgate, and Longues with 770 Lancaster, Halifax, and Stirling bombers.

4 Between 0443hrs and 0557hrs, IX Bomber Command, US Ninth Air Force bombs coastal batteries at Houlgate, Ouistreham, Pont du Hoc, and Maisy with 39 B-26 medium bombers.

5 At 0600hrs, IX Bomber Command, US Ninth Air Force attacks German defenses on Cotentin Peninsula, via Utah Beach, with 300 B-26 medium bombers. This is the most effective attack of the morning's missions. Simultaneously, 16 B-26 bombers attack an artillery battery at Montfairville.

6 The Eighth Air Force's 2nd Bombardment Division attacks German positions on Omaha Beach at 0600hrs with 450 B-24 Liberator Bombers. All bombs fall behind the designated targets.

7 At 0700hrs the 1st Bombardment Division, Eighth Air Force, send 422 B-17 Flying Fortress bombers against German defenses on Gold and Juno beach. The German defenses are not damaged. 66 B-17 bombers attempt to attack Caen, but cannot find the target and return.

8 The 3rd Bombardment Division, Eighth Air Force, attack German beach targets on Juno and Sword Beaches. At 0700hrs, 366 B-17 heavy bombers arrive over their objectives. None of these sorties hit their assigned targets. At 0746hrs, 96 B-24 bombers from the same division arrive over Caen, but are unable to find their targets and don't drop any bombs.

9 At 0500hrs Eastern and Western Naval Task Forces arrive off the invasion coast. By 0600hrs, the bombardment forces are engaging German coastal defense batteries and other targets on the coast.

10 Commencing at 0630hrs in the American sector and 0700hrs in the Commonwealth sector, five Allied divisions land on the invasion beaches. Only on Utah Beach are the German defenses neutralized.

The Joint Fire Plan

This plan was approved by air, ground, and naval commanders and published on April 8. It co-ordinated all supporting fires for the ground assault on the Normandy beaches.

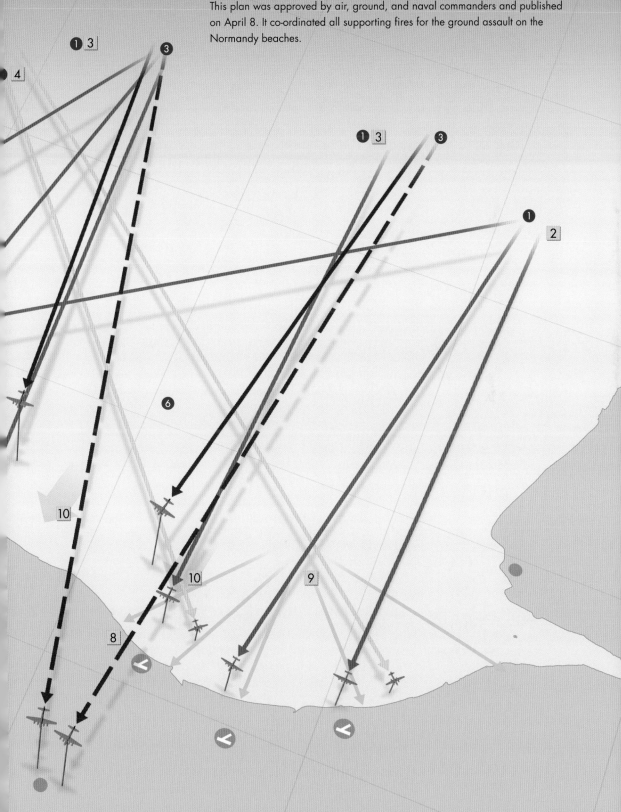

A British national hero because of his victory in North Africa, General Bernard Montgomery planned and commanded 21st Army Group and all the ground forces for Operation *Neptune*. He was determined to use all aircraft available in the direct support of his landing forces. His insistence on employing heavy bombers against beach targets ran counter to the doctrine and training of the four-engine bomber crews. (KEYSTONE-FRANCE/ Gamma-Rapho via Getty Images)

requires their engagement by air attack, though owing to their nature complete destruction is only likely to be achieved in a very small proportion of cases." In separate appendices, the planners identified what enemy positions they wanted bombed and when:

A- Batteries for air attack prior to D-Day.

B- Cover Plan targets for air attack immediately prior to D-Day. (The *Fortitude* targets not included in this list.)

C- Targets for air attack on D-1.

D- Batteries for attack by bombers prior to H-hour.

E- Targets for naval bombardment.

F- Beach targets for daylight bombing during the assault.

G- Targets especially suitable for fighter bombers.

This list does not include Montgomery's requirement to slow the movement of enemy reserve forces onto the battlefield.

Of course, even though the senior commanders and staff officers had an agreement, the Joint Fire Plan was a long way from implementation, and it now became the intellectual property of junior planners at all secondary levels. These officers had to allocate the hundreds of targets across France, Belgium, and into the Atlantic to over 678 air squadrons, with 12,600 aircraft of all kinds. They had to plan the flight paths so that aircraft would fly out on certain routes and would not, on their return, fly into other units heading east, or interfere with the dropping of parachutists. Naval planners had similar problems with planning and sequencing seven battleships, two monitors, 23 cruisers, and 108 destroyers and other vessels in the assault zone, and many others on the flanks and into the Atlantic. Their problems were, in many ways, even more complicated, since over 4,000 other vessels – sailing in darkness without lights – would be hauling troops and supplies to and from the invasion beaches. And before the landing craft could drop their troops, minesweepers, caught in the fire between friendly vessels and enemy artillery, had to remove mines and obstacles in the lanes to the coast. Planners from both the naval and air services had to analyze each target, determine the kind of munitions appropriate, and then match them with the potential ships and squadrons that could execute the mission. Finally, they needed to sequence these missions, so they took place in priority, at the right time. All of this had to happen in such a way that the landing forces would not be hit, by mistake, by the massive firepower aimed at the French coast. In the end, incredibly detailed targeting schedules found their way down to both ships and air squadrons. The prime planning consideration in the assault was continuity of bombardment so that the enemy forces would not have time to recover and reinforce. For the air attack, Leigh-Mallory's planners prepared a detailed *Neptune* Air Plan that spelled out the responsibilities for all of the aviation services.

The intent, therefore, of the Joint Fire Plan, was to ensure that "the maximum effort of the Navy, Air Force, and Army was to be concentrated upon drenching the defenses of this stretch of coast in a continuous rain of fire from the time the Assault Forces came within range until the time when they arrive at their objectives." This plan was not the final document, as ground and naval commanders continued to modify their target recommendations until just before D-Day. For each of the recommended targets, the planners identified the results they desired.

Merville Battery

Admiral Ramsay's planners wanted the powerful long-range artillery batteries bombed while the invasion fleet was approaching the shore. Out of the more than 40 enemy gun emplacements that could have interfered with the fleet, they selected the ten most dangerous, based on their positions, gun calibers, ranges, and overall importance. These installations were highly fortified complexes, and the bombing was intended to disrupt and neutralize them for several hours. Bomber command received this mission, and it would allocate 100 aircraft and 500 tons of bombs to each emplacement. The US Eighth and Ninth Air Forces would, later, attack some of these batteries. Finally, once they got within range, the Naval Task Force's warships would be able to take over the suppression and destruction of these dangerous installations.

On May 14, General Bradley, whose V and VII Corps would land on Omaha and Utah beaches, submitted his recommended changes to the Joint Fire Plan. In a formal, signed request, he provided the air planners with a priority of beach defenses they wanted the heavies to attack. Bradley's staff identified 11 artillery batteries, some that the Navy also wanted neutralized, 15 German defensive positions on Omaha Beach, and 14 on Utah Beach. For example, in the First US Army area (Omaha and Utah beaches), the objective was not to destroy the enemy installations but to *neutralize* them. The word "neutralize," in military terms, is a temporary condition, meaning that the defenders would, for a short period, be unable to recover their equipment, replace casualties, and provide accurate return fire. It conveys the specific condition that the army commanders wanted the air component to create on the ground. If they could not do so, the air planners needed to tell the ground planners before the infantry approached the shore. Bradley and his commanders knew that the first half-hour on the beach would be critical for the landing troops. If the air assault could disorganize the defenders for at least 30 minutes, then the infantry would be able to secure the dominant terrain on the beach before the enemy could cause them much harm. If the AEAF could not, the ground leaders needed to adjust their plans and tactics – before the troops boarded the landing craft.

A close friend of General Montgomery, Gen Miles Dempsey (left) commanded the British Second Army. Badly wounded in World War I, he lost a lung as a result of a gas attack but ended the war still on the battlefield. Commanding a brigade in the disastrous 1940 campaign in France and the Low Countries, he led a division in England and then a corps in North Africa and Sicily. In May 1944, he submitted his list of German installations he wanted the AEAF to neutralize. Across his three beaches, the heavy bombers contributed little to his landing. (Sgt Morris/ Imperial War Museums via Getty Images)

Two days later, General Dempsey, whose men would assault Gold, Juno, and Sword beaches, refined his request. Organizing his recommendations by corps, he requested 13 bombing missions for XXX Corps (landing on Gold and Juno) and 19 for I Corps (Juno and Sword). Again, some of these included heavy batteries identified by Ramsay's planners. Also, as in the case of the American sector, none of the army leaders were under any illusion of the effects of the bombing. With many having fought in North Africa, Sicily, and Italy, they were well aware of the limitations of air support. However, they all believed it would help with their assault.

One final aspect of the D-Day assault was Montgomery's intention to destroy French towns on the German line of march. He and all of his ground commanders, American and British, were fearful that German armor would be able to mass and assault them on the coast before they had sufficient forces ashore to stop them. By the end of April, planners at Headquarters, 21st Army Group, identified 26 towns they wanted "heavily bombed on D-Day and D-Day plus one to create road blocks."

Neither Harris nor Spaatz wanted anything to do with this kind of mission, and did everything they could to prevent it. But on May 20, Montgomery became involved and made it clear that stopping the movement of Panzers within the "inner zone close to the bridgehead" should be a high priority. But the air commanders continued to fight back, and two days later, Leigh-Mallory met with the Eighth Air Force commander. Doolittle was adamant that "heavy bombers were not tactical weapons." Tedder agreed, and argued that bombing the road centers was wasteful since planners had based it only on map surveys; it would be an uneconomical use of airplanes and would result in excessive civilian casualties.

However, Montgomery got the impression that the air staff was challenging his demand to bomb the towns. So, at 1500hrs, he called Leigh-Mallory and asked him if there had been any changes. The AEAF commander assured him and replied that "he stood by the plan absolutely and would resign rather than abandon it." No one wanted to confront the ground force commander, whom they all knew Eisenhower would support. That would be the end of the debate regarding the utility of bombing towns. It also ended the Allied discussion on the air forces inflicting casualties on French civilians. On June 5, Leigh-Mallory approved the final target list, which had not changed much since May 10. Air operations officers scheduled 26 towns – with their churches, shops, and homes – for destruction. Under protest, Spaatz and Doolittle agreed to obey orders to bomb villages that had little German military presence, but received the concession to drop leaflets warning the inhabitants of the impending attacks. Caen was on the list for that first mission on June 6.

The "air force" problem

However, the US Air Force and RAF leaders were extremely concerned over causing excessive friendly casualties due to the close-support bombing. For months, Allied bombers had been attacking targets, especially rail centers, across France and Belgium. Moreover, air commanders were well aware of how inaccurate their bombing was, which was already affecting the war effort. For example, on May 5, the French Committee of National Liberation, through multiple channels, warned Eisenhower that the resulting civilian casualties were adversely affecting the morale of the French population. Air planners had at their disposal thousands of post-bombing photographs clearly showing destruction far away from intended impact zones. Now Eisenhower, Bradley, and Montgomery demanded that these same inaccurate aircraft act like long-range artillery for the invasion. It made the bomber leaders – Spaatz, Doolittle, and Harris – very nervous. This was not the kind of mission that strategic bombing "true believers" wanted to perform, and the record is full of protestations from the bomber commanders. Most concerning was the looming specter of Allied soldiers killed by friendly aircraft in a large-scale fratricide incident. Such negative publicity might affect the American flyers' goal of an independent air force in the post-war era.

Once Leigh-Mallory's staff approved the bombing list, the army commanders at all levels prepared for the assault, assuming that the bombing would, to some degree, hinder the German defenders' ability to engage the troops when they were most vulnerable. In addition, army leaders were confident that the powerful American and British air forces would neutralize the German defenders. Briefed on this fire support, troops were satisfied that the enemy would be disorganized to some extent. No one ever indicated this would not be the case.

One of the best medium bombers of the war, the US Ninth Air Force had almost 400 B-26 Marauders available for operations on June 6. With a crew of seven (two pilots, bombardier/radio operator, navigator/radio operator, and three gunners), it carried 4,000lb of bombs and had 11 .50cal machine guns (one in the nose, four on the fuselage, two in the tail turret, two in the dorsal turret, and one on each side). In this photo, 26 100lb bombs fall in a string from a B-26 Marauder of the Ninth Air Force. This was the load the IX Bomber Command used on D-Day. (Bettmann/Getty Images)

THE CAMPAIGN
The invasion begins

Operation overview

One of the four H683 casemates with its 150mm gun at the Saint-Marcouf (Crisbecq) Battery. This complex was one of Bomber Command's first targets on D-Day. However, the raid had little effect and it remained active throughout June 6, fighting with warships from the Allied naval task force all day, sinking the destroyer USS *Corry*. The garrison fought with the 4th Infantry Division until June 11, when it ran out of ammunition and evacuated to Cherbourg. (Jean-Erick Pasquier/ Gamma-Rapho via Getty Images)

Allied air attacks in support of Operation *Neptune* had been going on for several months before June 6. They began with medium and heavy bombers destroying French and Belgian rail yards in March and April. The purpose of these assaults, referred to as the Transportation Plan, was to prevent strategic deployment of German reserves from the Eastern Front or Italy. Then, in early May, while attacks on railyards continued, Leigh-Mallory directed his medium and fighter bombers to destroy bridges, first across the River Seine. Then, towards the end of the month, he ordered the Eighth Air Force to do the same on those across the Loire. The 21st Army Group hoped that demolishing the bridges would further delay the German operational reserves, those already in France or Belgium, from reaching the coast. Then, in support of Operation *Fortitude*, the deception component of Operation *Overlord*, Eighth Air Force bombers began attacking German troop positions and artillery batteries in the Pas de Calais. These missions were intended to reinforce the Nazi High Command's belief that the attack would occur in the Calais–Dunkirk–Boulogne region.

Soon after midnight on June 6, the first bombardment of the operation began. As identified earlier, what linked this series of attacks was their unified purpose: to damage or neutralize the German defensive positions and artillery batteries so the ground troops could get ashore. As the troops landed and secured their objectives, the heavy and medium bombers would shift their attention to other targets – such as bridges, rail yards, and towns – further to the rear. None of these attacks were "strategic" missions. Much to the disgust of the bomber commanders, Eisenhower was using their aircraft as flying artillery in direct tactical support of the ground units – a condition they universally detested.

Operation *Flashlamp*

Because of its ability to operate at night, Bomber Command was extremely busy the night of June 5/6. Operation *Flashlamp*, the bombardment of coastal artillery batteries, was only one of several separate actions carried out that morning by Harris's Bomber Command. These actions included:

Operation *Glimmer*. Using Chaff, essentially small metal strips to deceive enemy radar, bombers conducted a convoy simulation, hoping to add confusion to the German intelligence agencies and indicate the invasion would take place in the north.

As the airborne troops were in the air, the command executed Operation *Mandrel*, a radio jamming effort to protect the assaulting force, and Operation *ABC*, with the intent of radio jamming Luftwaffe fighter control stations.

Operations *Titanic I*, *II*, and *IV*, designed to simulate three airborne assaults and provide diversionary cover for the actual drops. These included the parachute dummies, nicknamed Rupert or Oscar, that increased confusion among German defenders.

The main effort, however, was Operation *Flashlamp*, Bomber Command's most massive operation of the war to date. By the time it was over, Harris's bombers had dropped more than 5,000 tons of bombs on their assigned targets, "the heaviest load yet dropped during any night of the war."

On the receiving end of this ordnance were ten coastal artillery batteries. Planners identified five of these massive concrete installations in the American sector and five in the British and Canadian sector. Generally, about 100 aircraft dropped a total of about 500 (UK) tons on each target. Harris deployed 1,136 aircraft on these attacks. The pathfinders from No 8 Group used Oboe to mark the targets the best they could. The bombers used, in most cases, 1,000lb bombs, seeking to damage and disorient the enemy as much as possible.

B-17 bombers from the 381st Bomb Group, seen from the ground. This is a good illustration of the heavy bomber formation used on D-Day. (USAAF, Eberly Family Special Collections Library, Penn State University Libraries)

OPERATION *FLASHLAMP* TARGETS							
Time (CET)	Target	Aircraft Sorties	Aircraft Attacking	Tons of Bombs	Bombing Group	Aircraft Type	Civilians KIA
0031–0041	Crisbecq/Fontenay	101	94	598	No 1	Lancaster	42
0043–0100	St–Martin-de-Varreville	100	99	612	No 1	Lancaster	1
0602–0615	Ouistreham	116	114	649	No 3	Lancaster, Stirling	100
0414–0439	Maisy I	116	112	595	No 4	Lancaster, Stirling	61
0529–0549	Mont Fleury	124	113	607	No 4	Halifax	unk
0546–0603	St Pierre du Mont/Pointe du Hoc	124	114	713	No 4	Lancaster	unk
0431–0444	La Pernelle II	131	115	672	No 5	Lancaster	unk
0125–0139	Merville	109	88	381	No 6	Lancaster, Stirling	66
0445–0459	Houlgate	116	113	467	No 6	Lancaster, Halifax	54
0514–0528	Longues	99	96	602	No 6	Lancaster, Halifax	8
	Totals:	1,136	1,058	5,896			332

Crisbecq Battery

The Crisbecq coastal battery (3rd Battery, 1261st Coast Artillery Regiment), commanded by Navy Lieutenant Walter Ohmsen and located between Saint Marcouf and Fontenay-sur-Mer, was the most dangerous installation on the southern Cotentin Peninsula. Situated on a ridge two miles west of the coast and ten miles northwest of the Utah Beach landing sector, it had a spectacular view of the naval approaches and most of the beach area. Its primary weapons

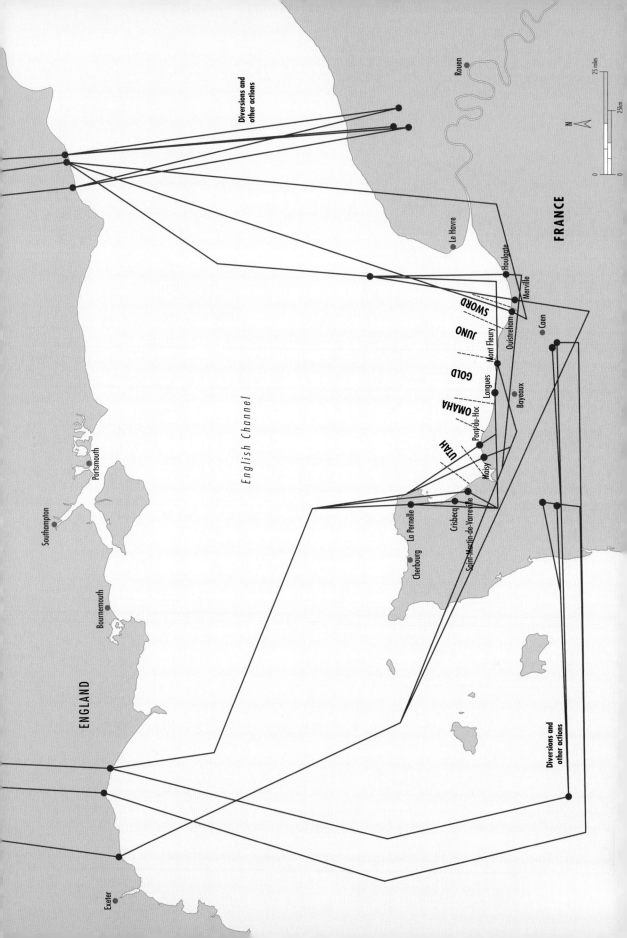

Diversions and
other actions

Rouen

FRANCE

Le Havre

Houlgate

Merville

SWORD

Caen

JUNO

Ouistreham

Mont Fleury

GOLD

Longues

Bayeaux

OMAHA

Pont-du-Hoc

UTAH

Maisy

La Pernelle

Cherbourg

Crisbecq

Saint-Martin-de-Varreville

English Channel

Southampton

Portsmouth

ENGLAND

Bournemouth

Exeter

Diversions and
other actions

N

25 miles

25km

OPPOSITE OPERATION *FLASHLAMP*

Shortly after midnight on June 5/6, 94 Lancaster bombers from No 1 Group struck the massive coastal artillery battery at Crisbecq. For the next five hours, bomber streams from other groups hit nine more coastal installations with the intent of preventing them from interfering with the Allied invasion force. By dawn, when the mission ended, 1,136 Lancaster and Halifax bombers had dropped 5,896 tons of bombs on these positions.

were three Skoda 210mm naval guns with a range of more than 16 miles. By June 6, two were in their R683 casemates; another was operational but not yet protected. The Germans planned to mount a fourth gun, but it was not ready for combat. The installation also had a Krupp 150mm naval gun mounted in an M272 casemate with a range of about nine miles. It had a robust antiaircraft presence, with four 20mm guns and six Schneider 75mm guns, as well as eight machine-gun positions for additional close-in defense, with mines and barbed wire surrounding the entire installation. Air Vice-Marshal Edward Rice's No 1 Group of Bomber Command hit this target at 0031hrs on June 6, with 92 Lancaster bombers dropping 598 (US) tons of ordnance. Just two of the five assigned Mosquitoes from the 8th Pathfinder Group made it to the target, so the bomb crews could only pick up a few of the target indicator flares. The crews reported light antiaircraft fire. The two guns in the casemates and anything else under concrete protection survived. The chateau in Saint Marcouf, where many German soldiers lived, took a direct hit, killing more than a dozen of them.

However, the bombers killed more than the enemy. The 120 or so citizens who remained in the villages of Saint Marcouf and Fontenay-sur-Mer went to bed on the night of June 5, knowing that the Allied invasion would happen soon. Everyone knew it was coming; the only questions were when and where? Many years later, Yvette Moreau, from Saint Marcouf, recalled: "Everyone in Normandy shared the hope that the landings would take place elsewhere. Farther north, in the Nord, of course!"

For two years, they had lived in the shadow of the German naval artillery battery at Crisbecq, less than a mile away from where many people had lived, farmed, and worked for generations. Veterans of the previous war probably had some foreboding of the danger they were in if the invasion took place on the eastern beaches of the Cotentin Peninsula. Then, soon after midnight, Mosquito bombers arrived overhead. There was no warning, and the sleepy villagers had to immediately choose between staying put in their homes or running

Concrete shelters, such as this one that still stands behind Utah Beach, offered German defenders some protection from Allied bombardment. (Richard Drew, Atlantikwall.com)

Navy Lieutenant Walter Ohmsen commanded the Crisbecq Battery and kept it operational for almost a week after its bombardment. After several days of ground attack by the US 4th Infantry Division, he exfiltrated his survivors back to Cherbourg. His defense of Crisbecq highlights the ineffectiveness of Bomber Command's attack on June 6. (Bundesarchiv, Bild 183-R63849, Fotograf(in): Scherl)

OPPOSITE
Air Vice-Marshal Ralph Cochrane, whose No 5 Group included the 617th Squadron, known as the "Dambusters" for their famous raid in 1943. His targets on the morning of June 6 included the batteries at Pointe du Hoc and La Pernelle. (IWM CH 14564)

to the shelter. In Saint Marcouf, the air raid shelter was in the church, about 300 meters east of the village center. Many never made it. Rene Millett, the mayor of the small town, remembered 50 years later the wounded crying for help and the sight of the dead, those who could not reach the shelter, lying in the road. Over the next few days, amid the fighting around them, the survivors would search the shattered homes and recover the dead. The Bazin family (Claude, Georges, Louis, Marie, and Valentine), the Carré family (Alexander Gustave, Alexander Louis, Juliette, René, Renée, and Thérèse) all perished in the attack. The Tixier family (Armandine, Etienne, Gertrude, and Michael) also died, and the list goes on. Forty-five French civilians, approximately a third of the population of these two villages, died that morning in the opening rounds of the invasion.

The battery itself not only survived, but fought a credible naval duel with five major US Navy ships (three battleships and two cruisers) until 0900hrs on June 6. One of the guns, incapable of engaging the naval targets, continued to bombard the Utah Beach landing area. Its commander, Navy Lieutenant Walter Ohmsen, working in conjunction with the nearby Azeville Battery, essentially stopped the US 4th Infantry Division in its tracks for several days, inflicting on it heavy casualties and requiring VII Corps to surround and isolate the position. On June 11, a week after the invasion, Ohmsen and his remaining defenders left the battery and infiltrated their way back to Cherbourg.

Saint-Martin-de-Varreville Battery

One of the older firing positions in the region, the 2nd Battery, 1261st Coast Artillery Regiment, occupied an area south of Saint-Martin-de-Varreville. It consisted of four Soviet-made 122mm K390 guns, with a range of about 20 kilometers, which could interfere with the landing on Utah Beach. Bradley's planners wanted this installation neutralized because they feared it contained larger 150mm guns. Another 94 Lancasters and five Mosquitoes from Rice's command attacked this complex soon after Crisbecq. Again, as in the previous mission, the crews could see nothing below – and they depended on the markers dropped by the Mosquitoes. This bombardment was a rare second visit from Bomber Command, whose No 5 Group had attacked this target a little more than a week earlier, after which the installation commander had removed the surviving guns and ammunition further inland. There, when the 99 aircraft dropped 612 tons of bombs on this facility at 0043hrs, it was essentially a wasted effort. Surprisingly, although the battery was just to the west of the village, the bombardment killed only one citizen, 50-year-old René Deladune. The US 502nd Parachute Infantry Battalion overran the battery postion, minus its guns, in the early morning hours of June 6.

Merville Battery

The third Bomber Command mission that morning was against the battery at Merville, east of the River Orne and guarding the approaches to Ouistreham, Sword Beach, and the

Caen transportation complex, manned by the 1st Battery, 1716th Artillery Regiment. Organization Todt, the Nazi engineering group which used much forced labour, constructed one R611 casemate here and three of the R699 type. Allied planners believed these fortifications housed 155mm guns, but each actually contained only a 100mm Skoda F.H14/19(t) gun, capable of firing a little more than five miles. Nevertheless, its location guarding the right flank of the German defenses on the Normandy beaches made it an essential objective for Bomber Command. Once the bombers passed, it would be one of the British 6th Airborne Division's primary objectives.

The assignment of neutralizing this critical installation went to Air Vice-Marshal Clifford McEwen's No 6 Group, the Royal Canadian Air Force's contribution to the heavy bombing war. For this mission, McEwen employed a mixed force of 86 Lancasters and 13 generally obsolete Stirling bombers. Only three out of the five pathfinder aircraft and a total of 88 bombers made it to the target. With the crews unable to pick out any of the target indicator flares, it is no wonder that most of the 381 tons of bombs missed the target, with some falling dangerously close to the 6th Airborne's pathfinders and reconnaissance troops.

The small towns surrounding the battery took most of the casualties, with at least 66 dead and probably twice that number injured. It is almost impossible to ascribe which bomb and which mission caused their deaths. However, the pattern of this mission, outside of the landing zone, reflects the results of a surprise, scattered attack. At that time in the morning, with no warning, the civilians would have been asleep and unaware of what was about to transpire. Located between the Merville and Houlgate batteries, the town of Cabourg alone suffered 28 dead. It is ironic that the battery commander, Captain Karl-Heinrich Wolter, was with his mistress in the town when Bomber Command struck, and he perished in the attack. Lieutenant Raimund Steiner took over command of the battery, and would defend it during the 6th Airborne's assault on the position. The paratroopers drove the German troops away, but they did not have the explosives they required to destroy the guns. Once the British withdrew, Steiner and some of his survivors returned and put the guns back into operation. Most likely reinforced by other German soldiers, Steiner and his troops manned the guns and withstood later air attacks and British efforts to dislodge them until August 17.

Air Vice-Marshal Clifford "Black Mike" McEwen had led the Canadian No 6 Group since February. The D-Day mission was not the Canadians' best performance, but his group would emerge as the best in Bomber Command by the end of the war. (Wikimedia Commons/Public Domain)

Pointe du Hoc Battery

Thanks to the assault by US Rangers on June 6 and Ronald Reagan's 1984 speech on the site to mark the 40th anniversary of the landings, no battery on the Normandy coast is more famous than that at Pointe du Hoc. Located on a plateau, high above the coast, the 2nd Battery, 1260th Artillery Regiment's four 155mm K240 guns, mounted in H671 concrete casemates, could have played havoc with the assault on Omaha and Utah beaches if they were operational. However, the Allies had bombed it seven times before D-Day, so the German commander moved the guns to the rear before June 6. The battery would be attacked twice on D-Day, both by Air Vice-Marshal Ralph A. Cochrane's No 5 Group and later by the US Ninth Air Force. Cochrane's 105 Lancasters added 713 tons of bombs to the already plastered plateau.

However, the crews admitted that the bombing was inaccurate as they could not see the target area. When the Rangers captured the battery, they discovered the guns in their rear location and that the bombing had damaged only one casemate.

La Pernelle Battery

The batteries at La Pernelle, Maisy, and Houlgate were the next in line, beginning at about 0430hrs. La Pernelle II was part of an installation that included another artillery unit and a radar installation. Located near the tip of the Cotentin Peninsula, Pernelle I had six 105mm French Schneider guns and was not a particular threat to the invasion fleet. Pernelle II, in contrast, had three 170mm K18 guns installed in open casemates without overhead protection. Capable of throwing a 138lb shell 18 miles, it could interfere with Allied operations on Utah Beach and the effort to seize Cherbourg. Cochrane's No 5 Group had responsibility for this mission, and struck with 108 Lancaster bombers. The crews could see some of the targets, noting that the first bombs were scattered but the later ones more concentrated. After ten minutes of bombardment, the battery and the surrounding area had absorbed over 670 tons of bombs. The bombing was not very effective, however, and after a few hours it was back in action. The battery would remain a thorn in the side of the Allies until the US 4th Infantry Division overran it later in the month.

Maisy I Battery

Maisy was a potent artillery complex located west of what is now Grandcamp-Maisy on the western edge of Omaha Beach, manned by the 8th and 9th batteries of the 1716th Artillery Regiment. It had three separate but related firing units. Near Les Perrugues, the regiment deployed six 155mm Schneider M1917 field howitzers in open emplacements. To the southwest at La Martinière, it had a battery with four Skoda 105mm howitzers in three type R669 casemates (the fourth casemate was still incomplete when the invasion began). Finally, at the Foucher farm, another battery with four Krupp 150mm SFh 18 field howitzers was ready to fire from camouflaged, but open, emplacements. It was also in this area that Colonel Werner von Kistowski established his Flaksturmregiment 1 with its 88mm antiaircraft guns.

Air Vice-Marshal Charles Roderick Carr's No 4 Group hit this complex at 0414hrs, dropping 595 tons of bombs in the area. The US Ninth Air Force would also visit the location later that morning. Although it was out of action during the assault, the Maisy I complex was firing again on the afternoon of June 6. Carr's attack had caught the Flak regiment by surprise and it was unable to return fire, but the unit was essentially untouched and ready for action that morning. It reported shooting down several Allied aircraft later in the day.

Also caught by surprise in their homes, French civilians from the nearby towns and villages bore the brunt of the casualties. The attack killed a dozen villagers hiding in a trench in Maisy, while in the nearby village of Géfosse-Fontenay, a bomb hit the Boudier home, wiping out eight members of this farming family. Explosives also fell in Isigny-sur-Mer, seven miles inland from the battery. Rescuers later discovered a house with five dead bodies, mostly children aged between six months and 12 years. In total, the British attack killed at least 61 French civilians and wounded countless more.

Houlgate Battery

Organization Todt established the Houlgate Battery six miles east of Merville, on a dominating ridge behind the beach. Armed with six 155mm French-made K420 guns, it could shell Sword Beach and support the Merville Battery with its range of 13 miles.

Two guns were operational in their H679 casemates, while the other four were in open emplacements. McEwen's No 6 Group attacked this facility at 0445hrs with 113 aircraft – Halifaxes, Lancasters, and Mosquitoes – dropping 467 tons of bombs, mostly of 500lb caliber. Unfortunately, the target marking was scattered, and so was the bombing.

Apparently, the bombing caused only minor damage, and the battery continued firing at Allied troops until June 19. The Royal Navy took control that day and knocked it out of action, but it remained in German hands until August. However, civilian casualties continued to add up. Dives-sur-Mer, like Cabourg to the west, was also caught between the Houlgate and Merville batteries. When it was over, it had lost 54 dead, while Houlgate itself suffered 15 dead. Other civilians perished in some of the nearby farms and villages.

M272 gun casemate at Longues-sur-Mer. Over 6½ft (2m) of concrete on all sides, including the ceiling, protected its crew from physical harm from heavy bombers. Nevertheless, the sound and shock of the massive bombardment could temporarily put the guns out of action. (Frank Toogood/Getty Images)

Longues-sur-Mer Battery

One of the most recognizable German fortifications on the Normandy coast is the battery at Longues-sur-Mer. Located on a high cliff on the border between the American and Commonwealth sectors, it had a wide view of the ocean approaches to the invasion area. Its four M272 gun casemates housed 150mm TbtsK C/36 naval guns, with a range of about 12 miles. The Tobruks mounting mortars, machine guns, and an air defense battery protected the installation. Organization Todt constructed a fire direction bunker on the cliff above the coast. McEwen's No 6 Group was allocated this target, sending 99 Lancaster and Halifax bombers against it at 0514hrs. The Mosquito target marking was haphazard, however, and consequently, the 602 tons of bombs dropped had little effect, other than tearing up some of the buried telephone cables between the guns and the forward observer. The guns were in action during the early stages of the invasion. Eight residents of the nearby village perished during the attack. The US Eighth Air Force would attack the Longues-sur-Mer Battery again a little more than an hour later.

Mont Fleury Battery

Located just west of Ver-sur-Mer, on the Gold and Juno beaches boundary, WN35A, Mont Fleury, had four 122 mm K390 Soviet guns, capable of interfering with the landings on

Le Hamel, Targets 5 and 7. Planners put Target 5 in the wrong place and missed the main German defensive position at Le Hamel with its 75mm gun that covered the landing zone to the east, where the 1st Battalion of the Hampshire Regiment lost its commanding officer and second-in-command within minutes of landing. (USAAF)

either beach. Two of the guns were in partially completed H679 casemates, while the other pair were nearby in a patch of woods. Carr's No 4 Group was allocated the mission to strike the battery, and 99 Halifax bombers dropped 607 tons of bombs on this exposed target. At least one of the guns continued firing after the bombing, and British investigators later discovered that it had fired all of its ammunition. Whatever damage the bombers caused to the battery, at least 11 local citizens perished in the attack.

Ouistreham II Battery

The port of Ouistreham and its heavy artillery battery was the last of Bomber Command's targets that morning. The 4th Battery, 1260th Coastal Artillery Battalion, manned four 155mm K420 howitzers, each protected in an R699 gun casement. With a range of just under six miles, these were potent weapons that could create havoc during the invasion. Air Vice-Marshal Richard Harrison's No 3 Group had this mission and attacked at 0602hrs, with 105 Lancasters dropping 649 tons of bombs on the target. But the target marking was once again inaccurate, and the 1,000lb bombs did only minor damage to the casemate. Ouistreham was an important port and transportation center, and the hub for the local tourist industry. As a result, it was well developed and populated. Unfortunately, the inaccurate bombing caused terrible suffering around the area. Almost 100 civilians died that morning, most likely during the early hours when still in their homes. Always missing in the reports is an estimate of how many people were seriously injured and required medical care, which would not come until much later after the British had secured the town.

It is difficult to judge just how effective was Bomber Command's most significant effort of the war so far. Unfortunately, the official Royal Air Force narrative of events that morning fails to address the ineffectiveness of this mission, carried out by more than 1,000 aircraft. "Physical damage to guns and casemates does not appear to have been very extensive, even when hits were registered near the guns." The report goes on to essentially distort the results, stating that German "personnel suffered so badly from shock that while most of them were disinclined to come out of their shelters many were incapable of efficient work even when they did man the batteries." In his postwar after-action report, Arthur Harris boasts that his bombing operation had "effectively silenced all opposition." Neither of these comments are accurate. For example, German defenders at Crisbecq and other batteries continued to fight until overrun by infantry days later. There are other examples of these installations effectively contributing to the German defenses.

While *Flashlamp* failed to silence the German coastal artillery, it was costly to the unsuspecting French civilians. The following day, many never emerged from their homes, perished running toward their shelters, or escaped with physical and mental scars from that experience. There is little wonder that Harris and other British aviation enthusiasts have not celebrated Operation *Flashlamp* among Bomber Command's most outstanding performances. Most histories of the command spend less than a paragraph discussing it.

To bomber enthusiasts, supporting ground and naval forces was generally considered an "air diversion." Unfortunately, unit commanders do not have the luxury to choose their missions, and, in this instance, Bomber Command was singularly ineffective. Now it was time for the Americans to execute the next phase of the Joint Fire Plan.

Eighth Air Force's tactical assault

On the eve of the landings, many leaders remained concerned about using the heavy bombers during the assault. For example, at the "Second Air Commander's Meeting" on

Ouistreham soon after the landings. Note the large bomb craters in the center of the town, caused by the explosion of 1,000lb bombs. (USAAF)

May 26, less than two weeks before the anticipated landings on June 5, Professor Solly Zuckerman, Tedder's scientific advisor, gave an analysis of recent attacks on the coastal batteries. He explained that Allied bombers had already dropped a total of 8,700 tons of bombs on these types of fortified targets in the *Neptune* and *Fortitude* area. Out of the 51 guns attacked in the *Neptune* area, they had partially damaged only 18, and of the 101 in the *Fortitude* area, only 26. The bombers had destroyed none of them. Zuckerman's calculations caused him to estimate that to hit one gun would take approximately 97 sorties and 420 tons of bombs. For the heavy bombers to have even one near hit, they would need to drop 2,500 bombs. Zuckerman was not reassuring to the Army and Navy leaders, who wanted these targets destroyed before they arrived. Moreover, the weather forecast continued to be a problem for the air commanders, and Tedder wondered if the attack could go forward if the bombers could not find the target. However, as noted earlier, General Doolittle responded with good news, and assured the ground commanders that if the weather conditions allowed his bombers to take off, they could neutralize the German positions along the beach. It was a bold claim, but his stature as the leader of the bombing raid against Tokyo convinced the ground commanders that they were in good hands. They accepted Doolittle's assurance and assumed the US Eighth Air Force would neutralize most beach targets.

Change of plans

Doolittle promised a relatively high degree of accuracy for his bombers. It is most likely, if he had been allowed to proceed as he briefed his peers and senior airmen, that the Eighth Air Force would have put many of the German positions in the target area out of action. While protected casemates may have survived, the attack would have damaged trenches, supply dumps, and exposed artillery batteries, and certainly stunned the defenders. However, that was not to be, and a debate continued among the Eighth Air Force's leaders and planners concerning the dangers of hitting the soldiers in their landing craft heading for the coast. Sometime after June 4, his staff modified Doolittle's concept. According to the Eighth Air Force's analysis of the D-Day bombing:

> When it became apparent that weather conditions would necessitate use of the latter, which involved navigating by GEE fixes and bombing on H2X Pathfinder instruments, it was deemed advisable to adopt further precautionary measures to prevent bombs from falling on friendly troops. (The time interval between the cessation of bombing of the immediate beach areas and the touchdown of the initial assault waves had been already increased from five minutes under the visual bombing plan to ten minutes under the revised overcast bombing plan.) Accordingly, in conjunction with Headquarters AEAF, it was decided that if cloud cover should prevent visual synchronization, bombs would be dropped on Pathfinder indications in the normal manner except that the release would be delayed so that the Mean Point of Impact would be no less than 1,000 yards from the forward wave of the water borne assault forces.

> With the revised plan, the H2X operator in the lead aircraft, who sat at a console behind the pilot, was to delay the actual drop. He did this by telling the bombardier, who controlled the bomb's release, to execute between five and 30 seconds, depending on the target, after identifying it. Since none of the trailing aircraft had these machines, the actual drop

Brigadier General Orvil A. Anderson had responsibility for planning all air operations for the Eighth Air Force as its A-3 or operations officer. He was instrumental in the decision to change the command's bombing plan on D-Day. Hardheaded and aggressive, he would have had little hesitation to overrule Doolittle if he believed he was right. After the war, he became the first president of the Air War College. However, the Truman administration later fired him because of his comments on using nuclear weapons against Russia during the Korean War. (USAAF)

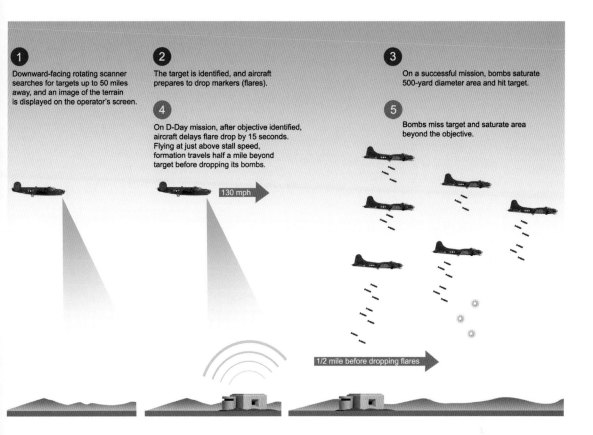

1 Downward-facing rotating scanner searches for targets up to 50 miles away, and an image of the terrain is displayed on the operator's screen.

2 The target is identified, and aircraft prepares to drop markers (flares).

3 On a successful mission, bombs saturate 500-yard diameter area and hit target.

4 On D-Day mission, after objective identified, aircraft delays flare drop by 15 seconds. Flying at just above stall speed, formation travels half a mile beyond target before dropping its bombs.

5 Bombs miss target and saturate area beyond the objective.

130 mph

1/2 mile before dropping flares

ABOVE H2X BOMBING ON D-DAY

by these crews would be several seconds later. Supposedly, this delay was intended to limit casualties amongst the Allied landing forces, but it also restricted the damage it could do to the German defenders. For example, a five-second delay would result in aircraft overflying the intended target by almost a thousand feet; a 30-second delay would move that target zone a mile south of where the defenders were.

Few details have survived as to who directed this change, so it is essential to review this command's decision makers. Brigadier General Orvil A. Anderson was the chief of the A-3 (Operations) section. Starting his service as a balloonist, he spent time in the Air War Plans Division and helped develop the fundamental American doctrine on concepts of strategic airpower. As Doolittle's operations officer, he had supervised the plans and operations for "Big Week," which broke the back of the Luftwaffe, and other significant air raids. Most likely, Anderson was at the heart of this decision. After the war, he would be the founder and first commandant of the Air War College. His deputy and another critical personality in this decision was Col Walter E. Todd. Todd was the deputy director of the air element of the Strategy and Policy Group at the War Department before joining the command in May. He later compiled a detailed special report in November for General "Hap" Arnold in Washington, describing the Eighth Air Force's participation in *Neptune*. Perhaps it is just a coincidence, but Todd would also become a commandant of the Air War College. Colonel Chester P. Gilger was another member of the operations staff, and director of tactics research, involved in the process. In July, he led a team to Normandy inspect the bombing locations and evaluate what kind of damage the bombing inflicted on the German defenses.

Providing staff supervision for the Eighth Air Force's *Neptune* support, Col Walter E. Todd was involved in making the decision to change the bombing times. An intellectual and strong proponent of air power, he supervised the command's after-action report that sought to change the narrative and obscure any responsibility for its poor performance. He would later become commander and president of the Air University at Maxwell Air Force Base. (USAAF)

Almost certainly involved in this decision was Brig. Gen. John A. Samford, Doolittle's Chief of Staff. Any contacts between the Eighth Air Force and the AEAF staff would have had Samford's blessing. He would follow Anderson to Maxwell Air Force Base in Alabama and command the Air Command and Staff School and the Air War College. Samford's deputy, who would succeed him as chief in the middle of the month, was Brig. Gen. John S. "Jack" Allard, one of Doolittle's closest friends. The two had been together on and off since flight school in 1918. In March, he had taken over as the Eighth Air Force's Deputy Chief of Staff, and there were few in or out of uniform whom the commander trusted more. This group and the colonels who worked for them, none of them with experience in ground combat, made this monumental decision in the middle of the night before the invasion.

Later, as US Army historians were compiling information for the *American Forces in Action* series, the change in bombing times caught their interest. The Eighth Air Force command historian was Maj Thomas R. Parker, who wrote a summary of what happened late in the evening of June 5. The so-called "Parker Memorandum" described how the planners became unhappy with their calculations on the evening before the invasion and worried about hitting friendly troops: "These officers were of the opinion that the overall results from attacks made by heavy bombardment aircraft in the assault area would be more beneficial if the number of bombs dropped along the shore line were reduced, and if a majority of them should be dropped in the communications and reserve areas behind the beaches proper."

These planners did not consult any of the commanders, who were already at sea. Essentially, Anderson and Todd, not named in the memo, overruled the decisions of Doolittle and the specific target requests by Bradley and Dempsey. Parker concluded his report: "Further studies are in progress at this headquarters and it is hoped that in the near future more specific information will be available." Unfortunately, there was no additional information, and no one in the US Air Force ever accepted responsibility for making this decision. No paper trail exists that can shed light on the decision-making process. Therefore, Parker's interpretation of events, certainly written with the help of the operations staff, entered the official narrative and became part of the US Air Force's official history of the conflict.

So far, the memorandum accurately reflected what happened. However, one paragraph is a severe distortion: "This decision was taken up with the Commanding Generals, Supreme Headquarters Allied Expeditionary Forces, and Allied Expeditionary Air Force... This change in the original plan, although coming at the last moment, was made with the approval of those headquarters to which the Eighth Air Force was responsible." Unfortunately, that is not accurate as neither Eisenhower nor anyone at Leigh-Mallory's headquarters approved this change.

After deciding to execute *Neptune*, Eisenhower spent the day watching ships load in Portsmouth harbor, ate lunch, and played checkers with his aide, Harry Butcher. Then, in the late afternoon, they headed to the 101st Airborne Division and had a series of highly photographed meetings with the paratroopers getting ready to take off for their assault. Finally, Eisenhower met with the press reporters assigned to his headquarters about the upcoming assault. The only issues of consequence he labored over that day had to do with the French government and the role of Charles DeGaulle, and the political aspects of the invasion. We should remember that Dwight D. Eisenhower thrived in his position as Supreme Allied Commander because he never made decisions, at least at this stage of the campaign, without consulting all of the concerned parties from both nations. Therefore, there is no evidence in any archival repository, amongst the thousands of documents, that he received a written message or held a meeting on this topic.

While Leigh-Mallory, the AEAF commander, perished in an aircraft before writing his memoirs, his deputy, Hoyt Vandenberg, maintained a detailed diary. That night, Vandenberg and Spaatz stopped into the AEAF battle room and noted that "everything was going according to plan." Because of his contacts in the Eighth Air Force's headquarters, he would have known about the change and was easily reachable. Even more ominous, although he had promised his fellow ground commanders that he would deliver most

of the bombs on target, General Doolittle confirmed in his memoirs that he did not know about the change until later. Bradley, commanding the US First Army, was surprised and unhappy when he learned about the change several days after June 6.

The assertion that the staff contacted Eisenhower and the AEAF commander is a brazen lie. No one from that headquarters ever briefed Eisenhower or his Chief of Staff, Beddel-Smith, on this fundamental change to the Joint Fire Plan. The only indication that the AEAF knew about this change is the copy of the field order they received soon after midnight on June 6. Unfortunately for history, Parker's report became the accepted version.

Just after midnight on June 6, Anderson's staff issued a revised order: Field Order 727 "B" (Plan B). Its purpose was "to cause maximum destruction and neutralization of these objectives in support of assault troops landing in the target area." Generally, this order was the same as in the original. However, the order now added instructions adjusting the bombing guidance. The exact attack time now depended on when the aircraft arrived at the target, and the relationship to the approaching troops in their landing craft. Based on this relationship, the bombardiers, as we have seen, were to delay the drop from between five and 30 seconds to ensure they bombed no friendly forces by accident. The consequences of these instructions for those landing on the beaches were catastrophic. With an aircraft traveling at 130–150mph, a 15-second delay would mean that bombs landed a full half-mile from the intended target. While no Allied soldiers would be hit during this bomb run, neither would the German defenders. None of the targets would be destroyed or neutralized, as the order specified. At 0100hrs, this order went into

Brigadier General John A. Samford was Doolittle's chief of staff and would have been the officer responsible for contacting the AEAF and Eisenhower's headquarters. However, there is no evidence he ever did. He followed Anderson to the Air Command and Staff School. He would later become director of the National Security Agency. (NSA)

An impressive display of the capabilities of this heavy bomber, a 490th Group B-24. However, it was inaccurate for tactical operations and did little to prevent American casualties on Omaha Beach on June 6. (USAAF, Eberly Family Special Collections Library, Penn State University Libraries)

Major General James P. Hodges commanded the 2nd Bombardment Division, responsible for neutralizing targets on Omaha Beach. Complying with his order on delaying the bombing by seconds, the division hit none of the German positions. As a result, the US 16th and 116th Infantry Regiments took horrendous losses that morning. (USAAF)

effect. No one ever owned up to making this decision, and, so far, no paper trail exists documenting the decision and approval process. The first time anyone realized that the mission was a failure was when the landing craft ramps dropped on Omaha, Gold, Juno, and Sword beaches.

Another Air Force historian who worked with Parker during Operation *Overlord* was Robert H. George, of the US Ninth Air Force. He wrote the chapter on the Air Force during the invasion in Craven and Cate's official history, published in 1951. George stated, based on the Parker Memorandum, that the decision was made "in the interest of greater safety and with Eisenhower's approval." Parker never mentions that Eisenhower gave his consent, just that there was consultation between staff officers. Was this George's addition, or does it reflect the influence of someone else in the Air Force chain of command? All of the participants were still on active duty and influential, and might have been able to review this part of the book. Since then, this incorrect account has appeared in the many books and articles published about the invasion. As recently as 2013, the distinguished journalist and historian Rick Atkinson wrote that the purpose of the Eighth Air Force's bombing was "to neutralize the German defenders beneath the weight of metal… And, on the evening of June 5, [Eisenhower] authorized another abrupt change requested by Eighth Air Force." But that was not so. In reality, Bradley and Dempsey wanted the German fighting positions neutralized, and Eisenhower never approved the Eighth Air Force's staff decision. The result would be effective German machine-gun and artillery fire killing and wounding American, British, and Canadian soldiers on four invasion beaches.

Omaha Beach (2nd Bomb Division)

Doolittle's planners selected Maj Gen James P. Hodges' 2nd Bomb Division for the task of neutralizing the German positions on Omaha Beach. His five wings were all equipped with B-24 Liberator heavy bombers.

Overall mission

The German defenses on Omaha Beach had been under intense Allied scrutiny since COSSAC selected this as the American landing sector in July 1943. Omar Bradley arrived to take command of the First US Army later that fall. Initially, this was the only American beach, and the army and Maj Gen Leonard T. Gerow's V Corps staff had spent months gathering intelligence on German activity in this sector.

Characterized by high bluffs opposite vast stretches of coastal sand, especially at low tide, this sector was difficult to attack. The key to American success was four natural corridors that allowed units on the beach to move to the higher ground in the rear. Therefore, securing these exits that allowed the movement of follow-on forces and supplies away from the landing area was the V Corps' first task. Conversely, the German Seventh Army staff could read maps just as well as the Americans, and they thus developed defensive pockets to deny beach egress and defeat any landings in the area. Therefore, these critical nodes were the focus of Bradley's target request to AEAF headquarters in May. In addition, he asked for strikes on two other groups of enemy positions on either flank that could affect the landing.

Under Field Order 727, Hodges launched 75 squadrons of six aircraft each – 450 aircraft in all – to attack and neutralize these 13 targets. However, under "Plan B," all of these bombers dropped their loads beyond the designated targets, missing all defensive positions. In all cases, the German infantry and artillery were able to fire at the American troops as they came ashore. Missing the strongpoints at Vierville-sur-Mer and Colleville-sur-Mer was exceptionally costly.

2ND BOMB DIVISION TARGETS					
FO 727 ChartNo	Target	Total Sorties	Attacking	Combat Wing	Bomb Groups
35	Pointe et Raz de la Percée	37	24	20th	(446,) 93, 446, 448
36	Strongpoint Vierville-sur-Mer	36	29	20th	93, 446, 448
37	Strongpoint Vierville-sur-Mer	36	33	20th	93, 446, 448
38	Hamel au Prêtre (Vierville-sur-Mer)	30	22	20th, 2nd	389, 445, 446
39	Strongpoint St Laurent-sur-Mer	38	34	2nd	389, 445
40	Strongpoint St Laurent-sur-Mer	38	33	2nd	453
41	St Laurent-sur-Mer le Ruquet E-1 coast	36	32	2nd, 14th	44, 389, 392, 492
42	St Laurent-sur-Mer le Ruquet E-1 bluff	36	21	14th	44, 392, 492
43	Colleville E-3 draw (West)	36	23	14th	44, 392, 492
44	Colleville E-3 draw (East)	37	31	14th	44, 392, 492
45	Colleville F-1 draw	36	17	96th	458, 467
46	Port-en-Bessin	36	17	96th	466, 467
47	Port-en-Bessin	22	11	96th	466, 467
Total		454	327		

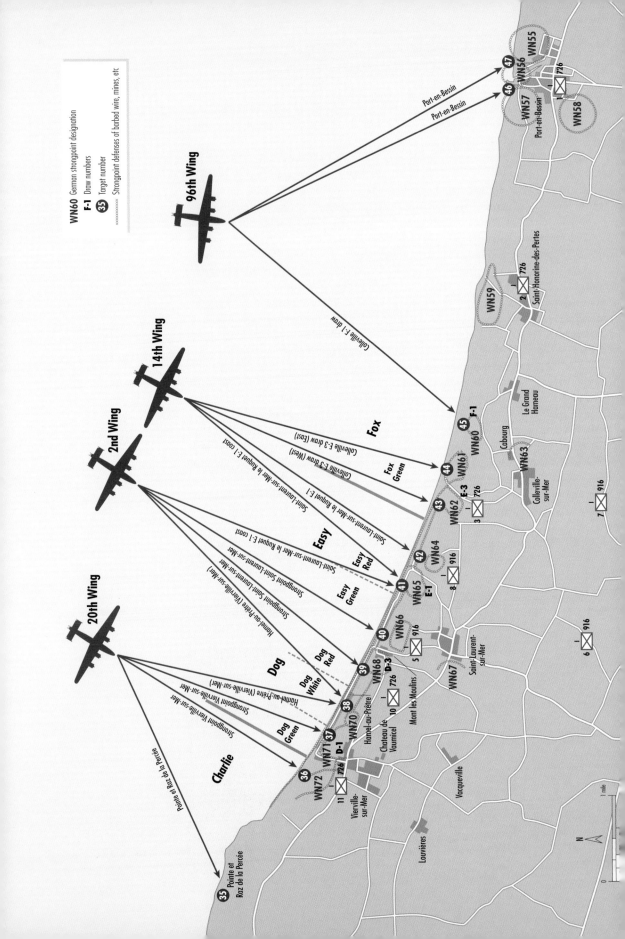

WN60 German strongpoint designation

F-1 Draw numbers

35 Target number

xxxxxxx Strongpoint defenses of barbed wire, mines, etc

96th Wing

14th Wing

2nd Wing

20th Wing

Pointe et Raz de la Percée

35 Pointe et Raz de la Percée

Charlie

Strongpoint Vierville-sur-Mer
Hamel-au-Prête (Vierville-sur-Mer)

Dog
Dog Green

36
WN72
WN71 **37**
D-1 **726**
11 726

38
WN70
Dog White

Dog Red

39
WN68
D-3
D-3 **726**
10 726

Chateau de Vaumicel

Mont les Moulins

Louvières

Vacqueville

Hamel-au-Prête (Vierville-sur-Mer)
Strongpoint Saint-Laurent-sur-Mer

Easy
Easy Green

10
WN66
916
5 916

WN67
Saint-Laurent-sur-Mer

11
WN65
E-1

Saint-Laurent-sur-Mer le Ruquet E-1 (coast)
Easy Red

42
WN64
916
8 916

Saint-Laurent-sur-Mer le Ruquet E-1 (coast)

43
WN62
726
3 726

Colleville E-3 draw (West)

Fox
Fox Green

44
WN61
E-3
916
7 916

Colleville E-3 draw (East)

45
WN60 **F-1**

Colleville F-1 draw

WN63
Colleville-sur-Mer

Cabourg

Le Grand Hameau

916
6 916

WN59
726
2 726
Saint-Honorine-des-Perles

Port-en-Bessin
Port-en-Bessin

47
WN56
WN55
726

46
WN57
Port-en-Bessin

WN58

N

0   1 mile

Vierville-sur-Mer, D-1

The most critical egress corridor was D-1, located near the western portion of Omaha Beach at the small village of Vierville-sur-Mer. It was the only paved corridor from the beach to the National Route 13 in the Omaha Beach sector. After World War I, the Piprel family had bought the land at the base of the road and established a restaurant, hotel, and casino along the beach. For those living in the much larger towns of Bayeux and Saint-Lô, it was a popular place to drive to in their Renaults and other automobiles of the era. Like most French towns, it had an ancient church, constructed during the 13th century, and a manor (Manoir de Vaumicel), built in the middle of the 1500s. In 1935, before the Germans arrived, the population had grown to 335 citizens.

Thanks to a persistent and determined group of modern researchers, we now have more details on how the German defenders developed their fortifications than the Allied planners could have ever hoped for. The 11th Company, 726th Regiment, 711th Infantry Division had responsibility for the defenses here. Three independent resistance nests (*Widerstandsnest*, or WN) controlled access to the draw, each with one non-commissioned officer and between 12 and 14 enlisted soldiers. From the beach perspective, standing opposite the draw, the hill to the west was WN73. Its most dominating feature was a 75mm Fk231 gun (French 75mm) gun dug into the side of the cliff, oriented to the east. Near the top of the hill, camouflaged and in entrenchments of Tobruks, were several machine guns and at least two mortars. Looking to the high ground to the east, soldiers on the beach would receive fire from several machine guns and mortars from WN71. However, when they looked straight ahead, they faced the most deadly defensive position on the entire beach, WN72. An antitank ditch blocked all access from the beach to the causeway. Behind it, an R677 reinforced casemate housed an 88mm Pak 43 antitank gun oriented

Behind a tank ditch, a R677 casemate housed an 88mm Pak 43 antitank gun, oriented east down the length of Omaha Beach. Historian Steven Zaloga called this structure a "Concrete King Tiger." Solid concrete and camouflage protected it from both observation and fire from ships at sea. It destroyed any vehicles that made the mistake of crossing its line of fire. (US Army)

3rd Division B-24 dropping bombs. (Eighth Air Force Archive, Penn State)

east down the length of Omaha Beach. Solid concrete and camouflage protected it from both observation and fire from ships at sea. A 50mm Pak 38 (L/60) gun, mounted in another casemate, protected the rear of the antitank gun. Adding more firepower to the rear of that casemate was a Tobruk-mounted French FT-17 turret, probably firing an 8mm Hotchkiss machine gun.

In addition, tied in with the defenses at the D-1 exit, another position (WN74) on the cliffs of Raz de la Percée gave the defenders observation of the approach to the western end of Omaha Beach. Designed primarily as a radar and observation post, it also protected a naval radar station. Weapons included an antiaircraft battery, machine guns, and possibly several field guns. Finally, defending this sector, both the 352nd and 177th Infantry Divisions had several artillery batteries within range of the Vierville strongpoint. They had forward observers to adjust fire, and most of the fire direction details already worked out and, in some cases, preregistered. This was an extremely lethal complex, requiring neutralization if the infantry was to get ashore with limited casualties.

There was little the air force could do about the massive bunkers at the base of the draw. The gun emplaced on the side of the hill was also beyond the ability of the bombers to destroy. The best they could hope for was to shock and mentally dislocate the soldiers inside. However, the machine guns, mortars, and troops in the trenches would have had difficulty carrying out their duties if the munitions had landed where Bradley wanted them. The planners identified two locations at Vierville for Colonel Jack W. Wood's 20th Combat Wing: Target 36 to the west above the draw and Target 37 at the base. The first B-24 appeared overhead at 0606hrs, and for the next ten minutes, 72 bombers dropped 213 tons of bombs when it was over, tearing up the terrain a half-mile beyond the beach area. They had damaged none of the enemy defenses and neutralized none of the positions. The German defenders of the 11th Company were ready to fight. Wood also sent six squadrons (37 aircraft in all) to attack the bluffs at Raz de la Percée, marked Target 35. From the French perspective, it appeared that most of the ordnance fell beyond the town, hitting primarily open fields.

This part of Omaha Beach was the Dog Green and Charlie sector, with the 116th Infantry, 29th Infantry Division, leading the assault. Joining this attack in the Charlie sector was a company from the 2nd Ranger Battalion. As the troops headed toward the beach, German howitzers, untouched by the air bombardment, opened up, creating concern among those on board. As the vessels moved closer to shore, forward observers adjusted fire. Two of the six LCAs (Landing Craft Assault) carrying A Company sank before they reached the shore. The other four continued in toward the beach, ran aground, and lowered the ramps. Suddenly a wall of fire engulfed this first wave. The defenders from the 711th Infantry Division, probably only about 45 soldiers in total, could cover this approach with fire. Machine guns and mortars, firing from three different directions, made any movement almost impossible. Within a few moments, all of A Company's officers were dead. A Duplex Drive Sherman tank from the supporting 743rd Tank Battalion arrived on the shore, and the 88mm antitank gun at the base of the draw destroyed it almost immediately. To the east of the 116th Infantry, C Company of the 2nd Rangers ran into

POINTE ET RAZ DE LA PERCEE

the same hail of fire. Mortars, machine guns, and artillery rendered most of this superb unit ineffective, killing or wounding half the company, 35 men in all.

Colleville-sur-Mer, E-3

It is doubtful that the 200 inhabitants of the village of Colleville-sur-Mer had prepared for the events of June 6. Off the beaten path and away from the National Route highway, their pattern of life had been relatively consistent since Scandinavians settled in the area during the era of Viking invasions in the 9th century. As late as 1930, the village's most prominent feature was the 12th-century church of Notre-Dame de l'Assumption de Colleville. They harvested typical Norman crops, especially apples that they turned into cider or Calvados' potent brandy. For centuries, villagers traversed down the ancient trail to the coast to fish and enjoy the ocean. At low tide, the wide sands allowed them to gather the plentiful oysters that thrived in the cold water of the English Channel. Unknown to them, the Allies named the old trail E-3, thus changing the village's character forever.

Lieutenant Edmund Bauch and his 36 soldiers of the 3rd Company, 726th Regiment, 711th Infantry Division, provided most of the strength for the three defensive positions that made up the Colleville strongpoint: *Widerstandsnest* 60, 61, and 62. In addition, an observation team from the 352nd Artillery Regiment, led by Lt Bernhard Frerking, and soldiers from the 916th Grenadier Regiment, 352nd Division, shared the position, bringing the complex's total strength to slightly more than 80 soldiers.

Omaha Beach, Targets 35, 36, and 37. Taken several days after the landings, this series of photographs shows the landing area at D-1, the Vierville draw on Omaha Beach. Target 37 is the German defenses at the base of the draw. Note the bomb craters to the southwest of the targets, far from the German defenses. Note also the early stages of the Omaha Mulberry Harbor, which a storm would severely damage on June 19. (USAAF)

EVENTS

1 0220hrs. Aircraft from the 2nd Bomb Division begin taking off and fly to one of four maneuver areas.

2 0730hrs. Within each of these maneuver areas, 18 or 19 flights circle as individual aircraft join the formation. Once all six aircraft join, the formation is ready to go. They continue to cycle until ordered south. The flights fly at different altitudes from 9,000–11,000ft, except for the 2nd Wing that circles at 6,000–8,000ft. Within each combat group area, approximately 19 formations of six aircraft are simultaneously circling at different altitudes.

3 0500hrs. The start of the assault is an imaginary checkpoint called "Point B." The lead flight in each wing arrives at between 0454 and 0505hrs in a column of flights. It takes about ten minutes for the entire wing to pass this point. As each flight arrives at this point, it is at its designated altitude between 14,000 and 17,000ft. The lead flight flies at around 16,000ft, with the next flights staggered at 1,000ft higher or lower.

4 0535hrs. From Point B, the four streams of aircraft continue to head south, flying somewhat

closer together. At 0535hrs, the lead flights from each column cross the coast at Selsey Bill, all in proper formation at the same height as at point B: 14,000 to 17,000ft.

5 0600hrs. Each bomb division begins dropping its ordnance on 13 German defensive positions across Omaha Beach. In general, the group hits each target with six flights of six aircraft each, from between 14,000 and 17,000ft. It takes approximately 18 minutes for each combat wing to finish its attack.

6 0615hrs. As each flight drops its bombs, it heads southwest towards the tiny island of Chausey, 11 miles off the coast of Granville, France, and begins gaining altitude. At Chausey, the flight is at 20,000ft.

7 0645hrs. From Chausey, the formation turns slightly northwest toward another small island named the Île-de-Bréhat off the north coast of Brittany and then turns north.

8 0700hrs. Island of Portland, south of Weymouth is the last checkpoint, and from here, the flights follow standard traffic control procedures.

Omaha Assault

The two regiments assaulting Omaha Beach (16th and 116th Infantry) and supporting troops began the day with about 6,200 men. When it was over, 2,500 were either dead, wounded, or missing. The failure of the 450 B-24s from Hodges 2nd Division to neutralize these defensive positions directly contributed to the high casualty rate.

Units:
2nd Bombardment Division (BrigGen. James P. Hodge)
1. 2nd Combat Wing (BrigGen. Edward J. Timberlake Jr.)
   389th Bomb Group (Hethel, Norfolk, Col. Robert B. Miller)
   445th Bomb Group (Tibenham, Norfolk, Lt Col Robert Terril)
   453rd Bomb Group (Old Buckenham, Norfolk, Col Ramsay D Potts Jr)
2. 14th Combat Wing (BrigGen. Leon W. Johnson)
   44th Bomb Group (Shipdham, Norfolk, Col John H. Gibson)
   392nd Bomb Group (Wendeling, Norfolk, Col. Irvine A Rendl)
   492nd Bomb Group (North Pickenham, Norfolk, Col. Eugene H. Snavely)
3. 20th Combat Wing (Col. Jack W. Wood)
   93rd Bomb Group (Hardwick, Norfolk, Col. Leland G. Fiegel)
   446th Bomb Group (Fixton, Suffolk, Col. Jacob J. Brogger)
   448th Bomb Group (Seething, Norfolk, Col. Gerry L. Mason)
4. 96th Combat Wing (BrigGen. Edward N. Backus)
   458th Bomb Group (Horsham St. Faith, Norfolk, Col. James H. Isbell)
   466th Bomb Group (Attlebridge, Norfolk, Col. Arthur J. Pierce)
   467th Bomb Group (Rackheath, Norfolk, Col. Albert H. Shower)

To the east, on the rise about 60 meters high, was WN60, also blocking a small draw the Americans called F-1. Four mortars, several machine guns, and a Tobruk-mounted R35 French tank turret provided close-in defense. Two 75mm FK 231guns, deployed in open firing positions, offered the capability to interfere with any landing. About 500 meters west was a small but powerful defensive position at the foot of the bluff, WN61. Like WN72 at Vierville, it had an 88mm antitank gun mounted in a strong casemate.

This powerful weapon looked west and gave it a field of fire that intersected with its sister gun. Supporting this position was another tank turret mounted on a Tobruk and a smaller 50mm pedestal antitank gun. Enhancing the resistance nest, the defenders prepared an antitank ditch to its front and then extended it west across the D-1 draw.

The most significant position was WN62, constructed on the bluff to the west of the draw. Today, because of its proximity to the American Military Cemetery on the heights above, it is one of the most famous and most studied defensive facilities on the beach. Its most notable features are the two R612 bunkers, each of which housed a 75mm FK235 gun aimed to the west, down the coast. It also contained two 50mm antitank guns, several mortars, and machine guns. Also in support were the 105mm and 150mm guns from Frerking's 352nd Artillery Regiment.

Brigadier General Leon W. Johnson's 14th Bombardment Wing had the task to neutralize two of these positions, those defending the E-1 draw, labeled Targets 43 and 44. Awarded the Medal of Honor due to his actions at Polesti in 1943, Johnson was a proven leader who Doolittle and Hodges could count on to accomplish the mission. Unfortunately, the planner's change in instructions complicated his ability to do that. He sent 73 B-24s against these German defenders. At 0600hrs, his heavy bombers dropped 141 tons of ordnance, mostly 100lb high-explosive and 120lb fragmentary bombs designed to kill troops in the open and destroy unreinforced structures. The bomb load demonstrated the division was

The three Eighth Air Force targets at Colleville-sur-Mer and the E-3 draw, part of a large panoramic display. Note that the only bomb craters are on the bottom left of the photo. (USAAF)

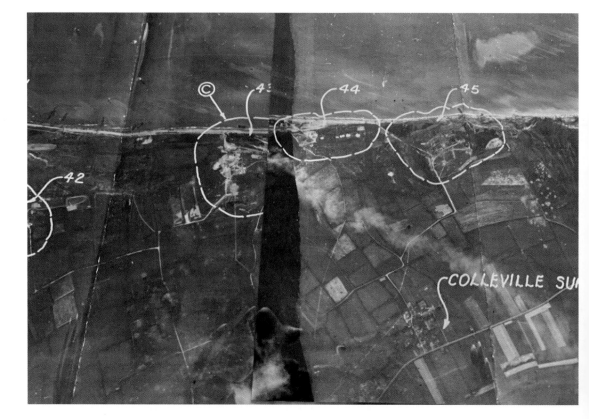

not attempting to destroy the bunkers but to attack the troops and unprotected weapons; in other words, neutralize the enemy. At the same time, BrigGen Edward N. Backus's 96th Bomb Wing attacked Target 45, the German defenses with the 88mm anti-tank gun, with 36 bombers carrying the same ordnance load.

Thanks to German survivors of the Colleville bombardment, we have a comprehensive picture of what took place at the defensive complex that morning. Corporal Franz Gockel from the 726th Regiment at WN62 survived the war and wrote down his remembrances of the bombardment. "The bombers were suddenly over us and it was too late to spring into the prepared dugout for cover. I dove under the gun as bombs screamed and hissed into the sand and earth. Two heavy bombs fell on our position and we held our breath as more explosions fell into the hinterland. Debris and clouds of smoke enveloped us; the earth shook; eyes and nose were filled with dirt and sand ground between teeth."

Private Hein Severloh was Lt Frerking's escort machine gunner and was with him during the air attack on WN62. He also survived the war and left a similar account: "Suddenly, we heard the dull drone of aircraft motors coming from the sea. The noise got louder and louder, and the roar of the motors rose to a hellish thunder as a powerful, ghostly fleet of bombers came directly at us in the gray, cloudy sky. Everyone jumped into the bunkers or shelters; I sought cover in my machine gun pit. Then, as quickly as they had come, the broad waves of heavy bombers passed over our heads, and were gone. Immediately thereafter, their load came howling, whistling, and crashing down. The bombs fell like heavy rain, and the first hit barely fifty meters behind our strongpoint. Everything started to shake, even our small, dug-in observation post vibrated from the detonations, and earth and chunks of limestone fell around close to us – but the bombers missed their target." Severloh goes on in his memoir to describe how Frerking was in almost instant contact with his intact battery of 105mm guns in the rear. The Germans watched as the American bombers flew away, and took cover again as the US Navy began shelling the Colleville strongpoint. However, with the defenses essentially untouched, the German defenders were prepared to defend the E-1 draw.

During a critique a week later, BrigGen Johnson, the 14th Bomb Wing's commander, reflected: "I thought our plan worked out pretty well, personally." It had been a classic milk run, although on a vast scale, for the crews of the 14th Bomb Wing. Unfortunately, that was not the case on the ground. There are few battlefields where the experiences of individual

WN62

A little after 0600hrs, 35 German soldiers from the 352nd and 716th Infantry Divisions were manning their positions at *Widerstandsnest* 62, one of three defensive positions blocking the trail to Colleville-sur-Mer. Today, this complex is a short walk from the American Military Cemetery on the heights above. It is one of the most famous and most studied defensive facilities on the beach. Its most notable features are the two R612 bunkers, each housing a 75mm FK235 gun aimed to the west, down the coast. It also contained two 50mm antitank guns, several mortars, and machine guns. The soldiers had been on alert since 0200hrs and were looking out to sea in anticipation. Suddenly, BrigGen Leon W. Johnson's 14th Bomb Wing, with 54 B-17 bombers, appeared overhead. Everyone jumped inside their tunnels and concrete bunkers, seeking shelter from the more than 130 tons of bombs landing around them. The bombardment seemed to go on forever as the explosions sent shock waves through the defensive position, shattering the soldiers' ears and filling the air with dust and debris.

Just as suddenly, it was over, and the defenders emerged from cover to evaluate their situation. Miraculously, the bombardment had hurt no one and not damaged their weapons. Yet behind them, the fields were on fire, and the bombers were beginning to turn west on their return trip. Lieutenant Bernard Frerking, the supporting artillery forward observer, picked up his telephone and was pleasantly surprised to hear the voice of his battery commander, a couple of kilometers away. Despite the massive bombardment, the line to the artillery unit was intact, and all of the battalion's 105mm guns were untouched and ready to fire.

This scene captures the moment when the German defenders emerge from cover and look at departing bombers and the burning fields behind them. One soldier then looks out to sea, points at the massive naval armada in front of them, and yells at them to retake cover.

Target 46 (near the "D" in the photo) at Port-en-Bessin. Few bomb craters can be seen in this image. (USAAF)

soldiers have been chronicled in such detail as that of the 16th Infantry Regiment at the Colleville strongpoint, and there is no need to retell these details here. In essence, L and I Companies of the 16th Infantry Regiment, 1st Infantry Division, were supposed to land on Fox Green, opposite the E-3 draw. In the confusion of the landing, L Company ended up opposite the German defenders of WN60, and E and F Companies, intermingled, arrived on Fox Green beach opposite resistance nests 61 and 62. When the troops left their landing craft, they ended up in shoulder-high water with no idea where they were. Machine-gun fire hit them, killing and wounding many before they even left their boats. The machine gunners and mortar crews had already registered their weapons, so the fire was accurate. The 88mm and 50mm guns had their effect on the landing craft, sinking several. Those defending this strongpoint were in the best possible situation as they were almost unable to miss their targets. It would take several hours and more waves of American soldiers before the 1st Infantry Division secured these heights.

An American infantry regiment in World War II had about 3,000 soldiers. By the evening of June 6, the 16th Infantry had lost close to a thousand soldiers killed, wounded, or missing. The bombardment had not worked out for these soldiers, many of whom might have survived if the 14th Wing had accomplished what Bradley had expected it to do.

Port-en-Bessin

Often missing from discussions of the D-Day landings is the village of Port-en-Bessin-Huppain, located to the east of the Colleville complex. Its history dates back to when it served as a refuge for Romans, Saxons, and Vikings. During the Norman era, it was the port for the city of Bayeux, at the heart of the Bessin region, five miles away. In the 17th century, the French military engineer Vauban constructed a small tower on the eastern side of the harbor. Constrained by its geography, with high bluffs on either side, it never expanded. By the 19th century, it had become a picturesque fishing village, often visited and painted by the Impressionist artist Georges Seurat. By 1936, it had about 1,500 people, and in June 1944 it lay on the boundary line between the British Second Army and American First Army. While its port was too small to land troops, it controlled the most direct route from the beaches to the critical city of Bayeux. Because of its rough terrain, the Allies intended to capture it by an overland assault, from the east, by the 47th Royal Marine Commandos.

The Germans installed three small strongpoints in the Port-en-Bessin area. Behind a seawall, 20ft high, two small installations, WN56, guarded the access to the port, with a couple of 47mm guns and several machine guns, protected by bunkers and barbed wire. On the high ground to the west was WN58, which had a 75mm Belgian field gun, protected by a casemate, with the capability to interfere with the Allied approach to the port area. Across the valley was another position, WN57, while the Germans had at least one other field gun positioned in the open.

The Allies identified two targets in Port-en-Bessin, 46 to the west and 47 to the east. Unlike the other 2nd Division targets, this was a village with a large concentration of French citizens. If the bombing was accurate, many of these civilians would become casualties. The 96th Combat Wing attacked the village at 0709hrs, with nine consecutive waves of bombers, 54 of them in all. However, only 29 could find their targets that morning and drop their ordnance in the vicinity of the port.

Fortunately for the village, most of the 46 tons of high-explosives landed in fields to the south, but not all. Twenty-five citizens perished on June 6 and 7, most of them from the American bombardment. The Calvados department's report on the Delain family, for example, indicates air bombardment as the cause of death for Blanche (49), Gustave (56), and Raymond (22). It also notes that Édouard (51) died when he was hit by a grenade, probably during the commando assault. The Gilger team of US Air Force investigators who arrived a month after the landings were able to examine both of the targets at Port-en-Bessin in detail. All of the fighting positions remained intact, and despite the tonnage dropped, they could find no evidence

Target 47 at Port-en-Bessin. The image complements the previous Port-en-Bessin image on p.60. Target 47 is at the top-right of this photo and Target 46 the top-left, on the west side of the harbor. Bomb craters are noticeable in the center of the image. (USAAF)

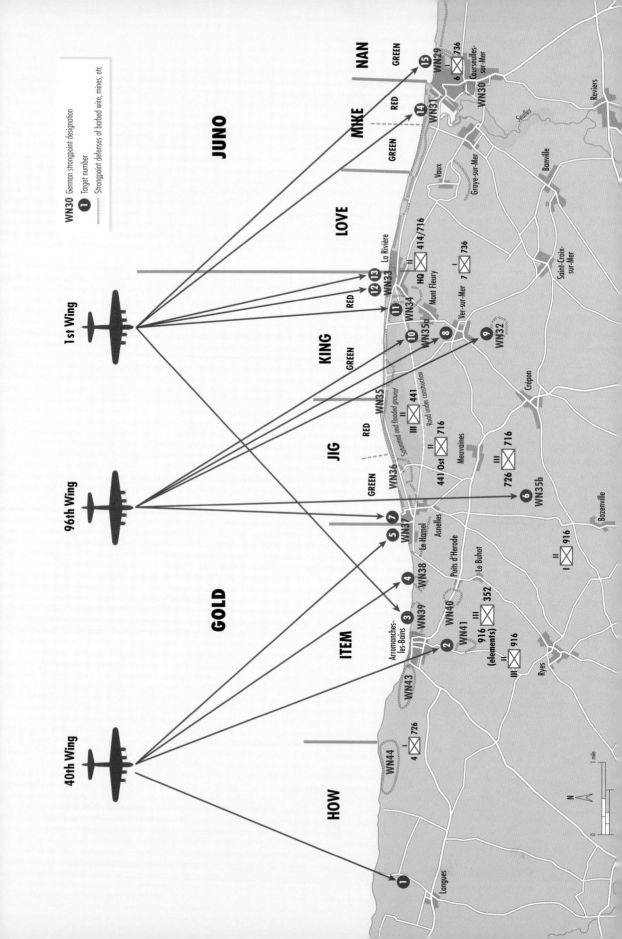

OPPOSITE JUNO AND GOLD BEACHES

This map indicates the 1st Division, US Eighth Air Force's attack on objectives in the Gold and Juno Beach areas. Three bomb wings, with 432 aircraft, flew this mission.

of damage on either of the resistance nests. Although the 47th Royal Marine Commandos surprised the defenders by attacking from the rear, the German resistance was tenacious. After two days of hard fighting, the commandos finally secured the entire complex, with the loss of almost half of its force killed or wounded. With more accurate bombing, perhaps fewer Frenchmen and British commandos would have perished.

By any measure of effectiveness, the 2nd Bomb Division's attack against the 13 targets on Omaha Beach was an abject failure. Four hundred and forty-six B-24 heavy bombers dropped more than 895 tons of bombs that morning. Apparently, this massive expenditure of explosives did not kill a single German soldier. Based on the effective small-arms and artillery fire directed at the landing forces at Colleville and Vierville, neither did it cause them to panic. As the day progressed, more and more waves of American soldiers from the 1st and 29th Infantry Divisions landed, greatly outnumbering the exhausted defenders from the German 711th and 332nd Infantry Divisions. The price was high, with approximately 2,500 American soldiers killed, wounded, and missing. Because of these casualties, and the drama of the assault, Omaha Beach has always had a special place in the American military narrative.

Gold and Juno Beach (1st Bomb Division)

Major General Robert B. Williams's 1st Bomb Division picked up the middle sector of the raid on the morning of June 6, attacking the towns and villages near Gold Beach, the objective of the 50th British Division, and the western portion of Juno Beach, where the 3rd Canadian Division would land.

GOLD AND JUNO TARGETS				
1ST BOMB DIVISION MISSIONS				
	Target	Total Sorties	Attacking	Wing
1	Longues coastal battery	36	36	40th
2	Arromanches coastal battery	30	30	40th
3	Arromanches strongpoint	40	40	1st
4	Arromanches coastal battery	33	33	40th
5	Le Hamel strongpoint	36	36	40th/94th
6	Meuvaines rocket emplacement	19	13	94th
7	Le Hamel strongpoint	24	24	94th
8	Ver-sur-Mer strongpoint	24	24	94th
9	Ver-sur-Mer coastal battery	24	24	94th
10	Mont Fleury coastal battery	12	12	94th
11	Mont Fleury strongpoint	6	6	01st
12	La Rivière strongpoint	18	17	01st
13	La Rivière strongpoint	30	30	01st
14	Courseulles strongpoint	30	30	01st
15	Courseulles strongpoint	30	30	01st
16	Caen chokepoint C3	30	30	01st
16	Caen chokepoint C4	36	17	01st
	Total	458	432	

Major General Robert Williams's B-17-equipped 1st Bomb Division supported the British 50th Division on Gold Beach and the 3rd Canadian Division on Juno Beach. The absence of bomb craters on the beach surprised the Canadian soldiers, who expected the bombers to damage the enemy defenses. (USAAF)

Miles Dempsey's British Second Army planners identified 15 targets in the Gold Beach and western Sword Beach sectors for neutralization by American heavy bombers. Headquarters AEAF also added two chokepoints in the center of Caen; General Montgomery wanted these turned into piles of rubble to stop German reinforcements. The army planners also wanted repeat strikes against the Longues and Mont Fleury coastal batteries. Within this relatively narrow sector, Dempsey attacked with two divisions: the British 50th (Northumbrian) Division at Ver-sur-Mer/Mont Fleury on Gold Beach, and the Canadian 3rd Infantry Division at Courseulles-sur-Mer. In addition, they requested several other strikes near Arromanches, which logisticians had scheduled to be the location of the Mulberry artificial harbor which the Allies would initially use to land men and supplies during the build-up. Williams allocated 450 B-17 Flying Fortresses against 16 identified targets. Against the artillery battery at Longues, he assigned 36 aircraft, continuing the ineffective bombardment of the critical installation. The fishing village of Arromanches had one improved resistance nest, several lesser defensive points, and an artillery battery. Against this complex he sent 103 Flying Fortresses. Other targets included German defenses at La Rivière, Meuvaines, Mont Fleury, and Le Hamel. The two most critical defensive complexes, discussed below, were the landing locations of the British 50th Division at Ver-sur-Mer and the Canadian 3rd Division at Courseulles. He also allocated 66 bombers against two crossroads in Caen.

Ver-sur-Mer/Mont Fleury

Before the war, Ver-sur-Mer was a typical seaside village catering to the increasing demand for the tourist industry along the coast. Besides its church of St Martin, dating back to the end of the 11th century, its main claim to fame was the lighthouse overlooking the ocean on Mont Fleury. In 1927, pioneering American polar explorer Commander Richard E. Byrd was guided by the Ver-sur-Mer lighthouse when he became lost at the end of a trans-Atlantic flight publicizing the US Postal Service. Other than this, the town is best known for its role in the D-Day operation.

The 7th Company of the German 736th Infantry Regiment defended three of the four positions in the Ver-sur-Mer defensive complex. At La Rivière, WN33 was the most powerful and well developed. Constructed on the coast, its anchor was an R669 protecting an 88mm antitank gun facing west. Mounted in Tobruks were two 50mm cannons, with enough of a punch to destroy light armored vehicles or landing craft. The position also had a Belgian-built 75mm Krupp howitzer in an open position and numerous machine guns and mortars mounted in Tobruks and bunkers. Behind this powerful position was a smaller enclave, surrounding the old lighthouse, with a 50mm cannon and several bunkers. The lighthouse was an excellent observation point, giving a good view of the entire coastline.

Widerstandsnest 35 was the other coastal position, located at Hable de Heurtot, about 1,000 meters to the west. A company of Ukrainian volunteers from the 441st Ost (East) Battalion held this minor defensive site. Its primary armament was a 50mm ring-stand-mounted gun, a Tobruk-mounted machine gun, and two 20mm antiaircraft guns. Both of these positions had solid artillery support with a battery of Soviet-made 122mm guns adjacent to Mont Fleury. Another unit of four 100mm guns in casemates south of Ver-sur-Mer and a battery of guns west of Crépon added to the complex's firepower.

Against the complex at Ver-sur-Mer, Williams sent elements of two bombardment wings. Colonel William M. Gross's 1st Bomb Wing attacked the La Rivière strongpoint, marked on the chart as number 13, with 48 B-17s from 0707hrs. He gave the other two targets – numbered 8 and 9 – to Col Julius K. Lacey's 94th Bomb Wing, which attacked with 30 more bombers. The two wings dropped a total of 220 tons of ordnance on the six defensive positions in the complex. No evidence exists that the bombardment affected any German defenders, although the air assault killed almost a dozen French civilians in the town.

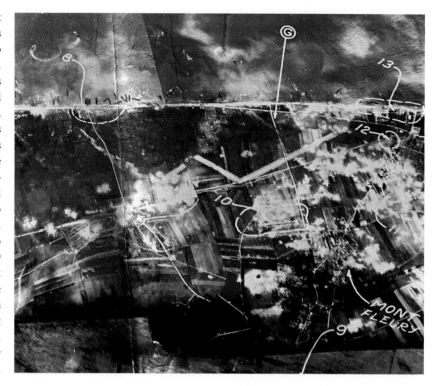

Ver-sur-Mer, Targets 8, 9, 10, 12, and 13. Note the bomb craters everywhere but on the identified targets. The exception is at Target 10. Most likely these craters are the result of naval bombardment. (USAAF)

Major General D. A. H. Graham's 50th (Northumbrian) Division had responsibility for Gold Beach. Fortunately for his troops, this sector was not as heavily defended as Omaha Beach, the defenders having weapons and a troop density of about half of that American sector. Brigadier Fergus Y. C. Knox's 69th Brigade had the task of capturing the Ver-sur-Mer area. His brigade consisted of three battalions: the 6th Green Howards and the 5th East Yorkshires in the first wave, with the 7th Green Howards landing later. Arriving in support were Duplex Drive tanks from the 4th/7th Dragoon Guards, who would help the brigade moved forward off the beach. At La Rivière, the 5th East Yorkshires landed directly

Juno Beach

At 0700hrs on June 6, 60 B-17 Flying Fortress bombers approached the village of Courseulles, a small port with about 1,200 residents. On either side of the harbor were two German resistance nests, the bomber's targets, manned by the 6th Company of the 736th Grenadier Regiment. Within an hour, soldiers from the 7th Infantry Brigade, 3rd Canadian Infantry Division, landed near each enemy defensive position, captured them, and moved through the town on their way to Caen, 13 miles to the southeast. The Canadians were counting on the 1st Combat Air Wing, commanded by BrigGen William M. Gross, to neutralize the defenders. However, changes in the plan, made by the Eighth Air Force staff, caused the bombardiers to release their bombs later than initially scheduled.

This view is about ten minutes into the assault, and crews can see fires burning in the town and fields beyond the beach due to the first attack. Some bombs landed in the village, killing 14 civilians and injuring a hundred more. While the German soldiers may be somewhat shaken, the American bombers have not damaged the German defenses, which are ready to fight as the Canadian landing craft arrive on the beach. The friction of combat forces them to debark 45 minutes later than planned. Both positions inflicted heavy casualties on the Canadians, who assaulted according to their pre-planned battle drill. In the war diary for the Royal Winnipeg Rifles, one of the two assaulting battalions, notes: "0749 hours. In spite of air bombardment failing to neutralize, RN bombardment spotty, the rockets falling short and the AVRES and DDs being late, C Company Canadian Scottish Regiment and RWR companies landed all within seven minutes. The bombardment having failed to kill a single German soldier or silence one weapon these companies had to storm their positions cold and did so without hesitation... not one man flinched from his task."

A 1st Air Division, 94th Wing B-17 in flight. Aircraft from this wing attacked targets in Ver-sur-Mer and Mont Fleury. (USAAF, Eberly Family Special Collections Library, Penn State University Libraries)

in front of the German defenders. Unfortunately, the bombardment had not touched the enemy resistance nest; its 88mm gun took out a landing craft almost immediately, and its machine guns began to take their toll on the landing troops. The battalion lost two company commanders, three further officers, and about 100 other soldiers killed and wounded within a short time.

The 6th Green Howards landed next to the Ukrainian-manned defenses at Hable de Heurtot, where the foreign troops did not defend their strongpoint with any sense of determination. The Howards then advanced towards the flank of the defenders at La Rivière and south towards the artillery in the Mont Fleury area, which the AEAF had labeled Targets 9 and 10. Thanks to sufficient armor and the fire support from naval guns, the 69th Brigade had cleaned out the Ver-sur-Mer complex by late morning. Compared to the American experience on Omaha Beach, this assault went relatively well considering the absence of accurate air bombardment. But the casualties of the 5th East Yorkshire Battalion would have been much less had the machine guns and mortars been unable to engage the landing infantry due to being bombed.

Juno Beach/Courseulles

Major General Rod Keller's 3rd Canadian Infantry Division had the task of securing Juno Beach, attacking inland toward the western edge of Caen, and holding the high ground in that area against any potential German counterattack. Three coastal villages – Courseulles (after 1957, Courseulles-sur-Mer), Bernières-sur-Mer, and St Aubin-sur-Mer – were the principal settlements along this stretch of coast. Courseulles, the most critical village, sits at the mouth of the small River Seulles. Historically an active fishing village, it had one of the larger harbors between Isigny/Omaha and Ouistreham. Among the other regional specialties, mussels grew in abundance on the rocks and quays along the river. By 1935, this port town had about 1,200 inhabitants and was unloading cargo from other small ports along the coast. A direct rail line to Caen moved the harbor's products inland. Sadly,

Courseulles, Targets 14 and 15, the major objectives for the 1st Air Division's 1st Bombardment Wing. The Canadians found no bomb damage on the coast, other than from artillery fire. Note the damage in the center of the town. (USAAF)

whatever history this charming village possessed before the war was essentially eclipsed after the arrival of the Canadian 3rd Division in June 1944. From then on, it was known as the center of Juno Beach.

The river and small harbor split the town into two sections. West of the harbor mouth on a string of sand dunes was a solid strongpoint, WN31, with a 75mm cannon in an R612 casemate oriented to the west. The 6th Company of the 736th Grenadier Regiment defended this position, also manning a second 75 mm gun, with 360-degree traverse, in a ring stand behind the dunes. Additional armament consisted of two 50mm guns, four mortars, and several machine guns, most mounted in Tobruks or other concrete structures. Barbed wire and mines added to the defenses of this resistance nest. On the east side of the river, WN29 blended into the town's seafront, just north of the rail station and its tracks. This resistance nest had three artillery casemates: one protecting an 88mm antitank gun and the two others a 75mm cannon apiece. It also had a 50mm cannon, several machine guns, and mortars housed in Tobruks or other concrete structures. One final position, WN30, was in the heart of the village, but had no heavy weapons. Altogether, this was an impressive defensive complex, with four casemate-protected field pieces and many small cannons, machine guns, and mortars in a narrow defensive sector. It was well-positioned to defend the small harbor which made it the most challenging area to assault, other than Omaha Beach.

Brigadier General William M. Gross's 1st Bombardment Wings had the mission to attack the Courseulles defensive complex mission. The 1st Bomb Division would attack the targets at Bernières-sur-Mer and St Aubin-sur-Mer, with 72 aircraft from its B-17-equipped 381st and 398th groups arriving at the coast around 0700hrs. The crews noticed a small break in the undercast clouds and saw some landing boats heading to the shore. Those in the trailing aircraft would have also noticed that no bombs were landing on the beach targets, all of them being dropped further inland. Despite the several concrete structures in the defensive positions, the bomb load consisted entirely of 100lb bombs, which would

Photographed by Air Force reconnaissance aircraft soon after June 6, Merville Battery's location near the coast posed a direct threat to the British and Canadian landing. This is part of a large mosaic prepared in July 1944, covering the 8th Air Force's bombing zone with each target marked. (USAAF))

not severely affect any such facilities. After dropping their ordnance, the aircraft turned right and headed to their waypoint to start returning to England. The total round-trip flight time, including forming up in the early morning, was less than six hours. The bombs did not hit the assigned objectives on the coast. However, they did strike the town center, where at least 14 civilians died that morning. Although it is difficult to determine who died from air bombardment, naval bombardment, or land-based weapons, many of the reports confirm it was often from air attack.

The 7th Canadian Infantry Brigade, commanded by Brig Harry W. Foster, consisting of the Royal Winnipeg Rifles and the Regina Rifles, had the task of seizing Courseulles. Unlike the Americans, the Canadians employed a technique called "Beach Drenching Fire," using smaller vessels equipped with artillery and rockets, and destroyers to suppress the German positions along the coast. This fire support was helpful when the Canadians discovered the American bombers had been of little use there like everywhere else along the coast. The soldiers all noted that there was no evidence of any German positions having suffered any damage from the bombardment. A typical comment from the post-invasion analysis was, "There was no apparent aerial bombardment."

The Winnipegs landed directly opposite the western position, Target 14, at 0745hrs, ten minutes later than planned, and suffered under murderous fire from the defenders' machine guns, mortars, and heavy guns. The 1st Battalion's commander noted in his war diary: "The bombardment having failed to kill a single German soldier or silence one weapon these companies had to storm their positions cold and did so without hesitation… Not one man flinched from his task." Foot soldiers defeated all of the strongpoints by hand, but at a high price. By the end of the morning, all that remained of B Company was the company commander and 26 men.

East of the river, the Regina Rifles received fire before they touched down. Nevertheless, the infantry and supporting armor were able to overcome the defenders. By 1035hrs, the brigade was able to report that it had captured its first series of objectives. However, the cost was higher than it needed to be, as the 7th Brigade suffered approximately 300 casualties securing the port.

Gross's 1st Wing was also supposed to attack two bridges over the River Orne in the center of Caen with 72 B-17s. Labeled Targets C-3 and C-4, only a few hundred yards from the city center, it was impossible to hit these without killing hundreds of French civilians. For this run, the cloud cover was too dense for the navigators to locate the city accurately. Consequently, the Americans dropped no bombs near the bridges on this mission, although the wing reported dropping 200 500lb bombs and 28 1,000lb bombs. Where they landed is a mystery, since those in Caen remained unaware of their threat.

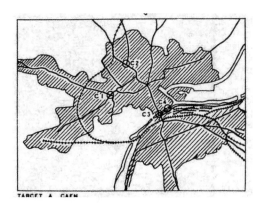

TARGET A CAEN

Caen target map, as reproduced in *Eighth Air Force Operations in Support of Allied Landings in Normandy, 2 June–17 June 1944*. It shows four checkpoints in the city. While they may make sense in the abstract, these were locations for historical and religious structures dating back to the 11th century. During the afternoon and evening of D-Day, bombers from all three air forces would destroy the city center. (USAAF)

One of the US Air Force's most aggressive leaders, Maj Gen Curtis LeMay had been the 3rd Air Division's commander since September. Assigned the task of neutralizing defenses on Sword Beach and bombing chokepoints in Caen, his mixed command of B-17s and B-24s was no more successful than the other two divisions in supporting the ground troops. He would later move to the Pacific as commander of XXI Bomber Command and direct the incendiary offensive against Japan. He became Air Force Chief of Staff in 1961. (USAAF)

Canadian historian Terry Copp noted in his classic *Fields of Fire* that investigators could find no evidence of bomb damage among any of the strongpoints or resistance nests on Juno Beach. He wrote: "No one who examines the events of the first hours of D-Day can fail to be impressed by the accomplishments of the assault battalions. Most of the elaborate fire-support plan failed, leaving the infantry, combat engineers, and armored troopers to overcome the enemy by direct fire." However, this assessment is not quite accurate. The bomber leaders did not fail to accomplish their tasks, they chose not to do so. Canadian troopers paid the price for the ignoring of orders they had received and promised to execute.

LeMay stated that: "The importance of success of this invasion is such that, if it becomes necessary, we will expend every airplane in the 8th Air Force to bring it about, to include use of the bombers to strafe the beaches." However, such words were just typical boasting, since his bombers did little damage to the German defenders on June 6. (Alamy)

3rd Bomb Division

Before he earned his place in history as commander of the strategic bombing campaign against Japan in 1945, Maj Gen Curtis LeMay commanded Doolittle's 3rd Bomb Division in Europe. LeMay's division was a mixed command of three wings of B-17 bombers (the 4th, 13th, and 45th Bombardment Groups) and two of B-24 Liberators (the 92nd and 93rd Bombardment Groups).

LeMay's task was to neutralize German military emplacements on the eastern portion of the invasion beaches – half of Juno Beach and Sword Beach – and bomb two targets in Caen to delay the movement of German reserves. Accordingly, he allocated 69 squadrons, with 354 B-17s in all, against the beach positions. In the 3rd Canadian Infantry Division sector, these

included the machine-gun and light artillery positions at Bernières-sur-Mer and St Aubin-sur-Mer, both major complexes the Canadians needed to capture to secure Juno. The British 3rd Infantry Division sector, Sword Beach, was the most developed and built-up in the entire invasion area. Before the war, it was a resort for Parisians and residents of other landlocked cities to escape to the coast. It consisted of summer homes, shops, and a casino opposite the Riva Bella beach in Ouistreham. The developed nature of the region, with structures built of brick, stone, and concrete – right up to the water's edge – made it a more dangerous sector. LeMay also assigned his B-24 bombers, 96 in all, to destroy two chokepoints in Caen.

As he always did, Curtis LeMay led from the front. As flights were still landing from their June 5 bombing missions, he called all wing and group commanders to report to his headquarters. He added in the instructions, "under arms." Colonel Thomas S. Jeffrey remembered that upon convening in the division's briefing room, the division's officers stood as LeMay entered. No one mentions it, but we should assume he was chomping on his ever-present cigar. He then laid out a map and began briefing the gathered leaders on the operation, timing, formations, and location of the attack. With the flash of brutal drama that was characteristic of him, he told the group: "The importance of success of this invasion is such that, if it becomes necessary, we will expend every airplane in the 8th Air Force to bring it about, to include use of the bombers to strafe the beaches."

There were no questions. On the way back to their quarters, they wondered why they had to bring the weapons. The answer, most agreed, was to protect the information they just received.

JUNO AND SWORD TARGETS					
	Target	Total Sorties	Attacking	Wing	Groups
17	Bernières-sur-Mer strongpoint	30	29	40th	
18	St Aubin-sur-Mer strongpoint	42	41	40th	92nd
19	Périers-sur-le Dan	12	0	40th	
20	Petit Enfer	24	24	1st	
21	Lion-sur-Mer strongpoint	42	37	40th/94th	
22	Ouistreham strongpoint	30	30	94th	
23	Ouistreham strongpoint	42	41	94th	
24	Merville-Franceville strongpoint	36	36	94th	
25	Merville-Franceville strongpoint	36	37	94th	
26	Manvieux coastal battery	12	12	94th	
27	Colleville-sur-Orne coastal battery	12	6	01st	
28	Ouistreham battery	12	0	01st	
29	Tailleville coastal battery	6	0	01st	
30	Saint Julien-le-Facon Div HQ	6	0	01st	
31	Bieville Regt HQ	6	0	01st	
32	Colleville-sur-Orne Battalion HQ	6	0	01st	
33	Tailleville 88mm battery	12	13	01st	
34	Caen chokepoint C1	48	0		
34	Caen chokepoint C2	48	0		
	Total	462	306		

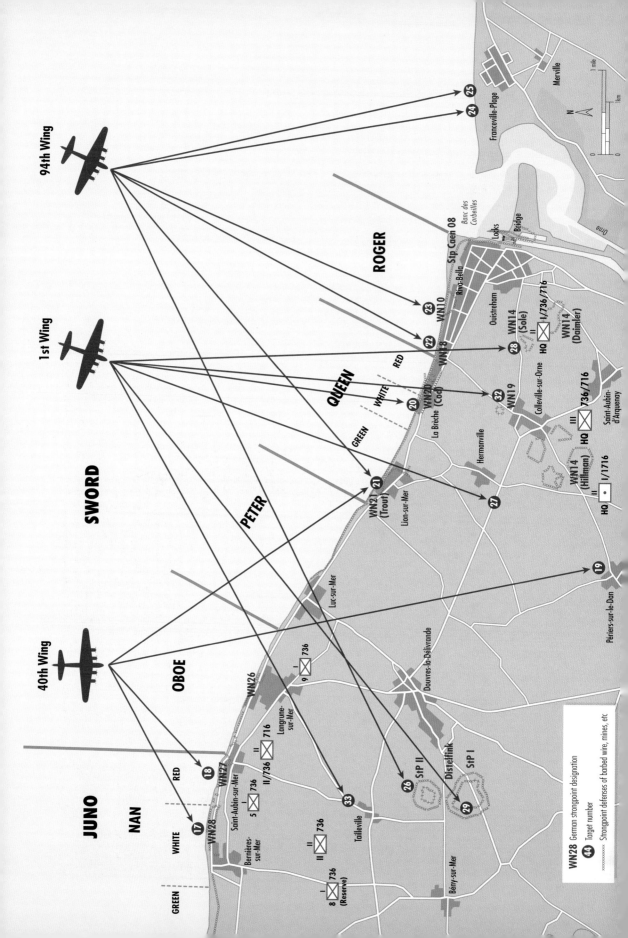

OPPOSITE JUNO AND SWORD BEACHES

Juno Beach

LeMay's two targets in the Canadian sector were the German positions at Bernières-sur-Mer and St Aubin-sur-Mer. Bernières is one of the oldest cities in this region, with Gallic and Roman ruins. In the early 20th century, its 800 residents played host to tourists looking to enjoy its sandy beaches. Two kilometers east was the town of St Aubin. Slightly more prominent, with about 1,000 residents, it was also a sea resort and home for tourists looking to get away from the hot cities in the summer.

The German 2nd Battalion of the 736th Infantry Regiment developed a resistance nest on the coast in each town. Neither one of these complexes was as prominent or dangerous as those at Courseulles-sur-Mer. In Bernières, the defenses of WN28 were rather weak, with only an emplacement mounting an obsolete machine-gun armed French tank, one 75mm antitank gun

Bernières-sur-Mer, Target 17. The relatively weak German defenders suffered little from the 3rd Air Division's bombardment. As is obvious in the photograph, many of the bombs fell in the heart of the town, killing at least 27 civilians. (USAAF)

Canadian infantry from the North Shore Regiment suffered 17 dead and lost six supporting tanks as it stormed the German defenses at St Aubin, Target 18, none of which had been hit by the American bombing. The town lost 25 dead and many more wounded from the 3rd Air Division's attack. (USAAF)

in a hastily constructed earth and timber bunker, a concrete-enclosed 50mm gun, a 50mm mortar, and several machine guns. The defenses at St Aubin, WN27, were about the same, with a concrete-protected 50mm gun, two 81mm mortars, several machine guns, and two 20mm antiaircraft guns. Because many of the town's structures were adjacent to the coast, the Germans often constructed their defenses within the original French buildings. While making them stronger, it also disguised the nature of the defenses from Allied reconnaissance.

The 45th Combat Wing, commanded by BrigGen Archie J. Old, Jr attacked Bernières-sur-Mer, labeled Target 17, with five squadrons of B-17s, some 30 aircraft in all. Each plane carried 38 100lb bombs. The attack took place at 0655hrs, with all but one bomber arriving above the town. Old also sent 42 aircraft to the German position at St Aubin, carrying a mixture of 500lb and 1,000lb high-explosive bombs. The Eighth Air Force reported that the 45th Wing dropped 168.75 tons of bombs on these two villages. With the landings taking place at 0745hrs, the bombing delay was minimal, so most of the bombs should have hit the defensive positions.

But they did not. None of the bombs hit the German defenses on the coast, yet many did hit the two towns. There was no warning for their residents. At 0700hrs, most families were getting out of bed, performing morning chores, and getting ready for the day. They had heard aircraft passing overhead for many months, so there was nothing strange about the approaching B-17s. Suddenly the villages began to explode as bombs hit the ancient stone structures. Bernières-sur-Mer suffered 27 dead and many more injured. These included members of the Bottard, David,

Huet, and Lequesne families. St Aubin fared little better, with 25 deaths, including members of the Hamon and Lebreton families.

In addition to these 52 deaths, it is estimated that between 150 and 200 more civilians suffered injuries of varying levels of severity. Additionally, many casualties, displaced from northern France or in hiding, were never identified. Given that naval artillery and Canadian Army drenching fire followed the bombardment almost immediately, it should not be assumed that all deaths can be blamed on the B-17s. However, investigators later noted next to a large number of death record entries the notation "*bombardement aérien.*"

While the bombers were killing French civilians, they were not neutralizing the German defenders. This part of Juno Beach was the Nan sector, the objective for Brig Kenneth G. Blackadder's 8th Canadian Infantry Brigade. It had arrived on the beach later than planned, at 0755hrs. In the lead at Bernières-sur-Mer, two companies from the Queen's Own Rifles were supposed to land on either side of the objective on Nan White and attack it from the flanks. Unfortunately, the wind and lousy navigation dropped both companies in front of the waiting enemy guns. While A Company managed to get off the beach with minimal loss, B Company landed right in front of a blockhouse; machine guns and pre-planned mortar fire, emanating from Target 17, killed or wounded 65 riflemen within a few minutes.

On Nan Red, opposite St Aubin, the North Shore Regiment landed at the same time. The defenders held their fire until the Canadians reached the shore. Then, as one lieutenant noted: "We found the guns and emplacement, which were to have been put out of business by the air force, intact and very much in use." The German 50mm gun, machine guns, mortars, and artillery began creating havoc on the beach. At the end of the day, the Queen's Own Rifles had 143 casualties of all kinds and the North Shore Regiment another 125. Added to this were the losses of units attached to the landing force, giving a total approaching 500 killed, wounded, and missing. Given the scarcity of concrete at these two resistance nests, accurate bombing would have prevented many of these losses.

Ouistreham

LeMay's next group of targets were in support of Maj Gen Tom Rennie's British 3rd Infantry Division on Sword Beach. Other than possibly Utah Beach, which was the start of the Allied route to the harbor of Cherbourg, Sword was the most critical landing zone in the *Neptune* assault area. Ouistreham, the port at the mouth of the River Orne and its adjacent canal, has been a trading port since the Middle Ages. The canal to Caen (Canal de Caen à la Mer) opened in 1857, and was improved and deepened in 1920. Fishermen and ferries to England used the port in the pre-war years. The railway brought tourists from the hinterland to enjoy the casino and spend time on the beach at Riva Bella. Its importance for the Allies rested in its short distance to Caen, only eight miles away, which was Montgomery's invasion priority.

Many houses and buildings occupied the coastal area, and German defenses incorporated these structures into each defensive sector. The critical positions along this short stretch of coast include a powerful strongpoint in Riva Bella on the canal and several resistance nests down the coast. The Germans constructed several additional defensive positions and artillery batteries south of the coastline, making a rapid advance to Caen a problematic undertaking. For this book, our concern is the defenses that faced the British infantry when they emerged from their landing craft.

The defensive complex at the mouth of the Orne Canal consisted of two mutually supporting resistance nests. Strongpoint 8 (Riva Bella) anchored this defensive line. Defended by the 2nd Company of the 736th Regiment, its main armament included a six-piece battery of French 155mm guns mounted in open emplacements, a casemate-mounted 75mm anti-tank gun, two 50mm cannons, and an R35 tank turret mounted on a Tobruk. It had a battery of 20mm antiaircraft guns for additional protection. Riva Bella was a significant defensive position, with some 31 separate concrete bunkers, casemates, or emplacements. Additionally, the Merville Battery across the Orne also provided fire support.

A short distance west on the beach was another resistance nest, WN10. Its main features included a bunker with six openings for firing machine guns, a 75mm antitank gun in a westward-oriented R626 casemate, and a 50mm cannon mounted in a covered emplacement. The 10th Company, 736th Grenadier Regiment, defended the WN18 resistance nest 2km west on the beach at Colville Plage. Another R612 casemate – mounting a 75mm antitank gun, a 50mm cannon, and another Tobruk-mounted tank turret – were the main elements of the defense of this position. Less than 2km west, WN20, codenamed "COD," was another strong position with a 75mm casemate-protected gun, two 50mm cannons, a 37mm cannon, a tank turret mounted on a Tobruk, and several mortars and machine guns.

A resistance nest at Lion-sur-Mer, WN21, completed the beachfront defensive positions the 3rd Infantry Division would need to overcome to establish its beachhead. Its primary defenses included two 50mm guns, a 75mm gun, and a 20mm air defense battery. In addition, many of the defenders occupied house basements, reinforcing the defensive position. The landing area from Riva Bella to Lion-sur-Mer was 5km long, with most landings taking place in a narrow 3km zone against well-designed German defenses.

Following the Allied raid at Dieppe and more than two-dozen other raids against French ports, the Germans learned to reinforce the main routes from the port with additional defenses. This was certainly the case on the roads from Ouistreham to Caen, with a line of resistance nests and artillery batteries blocking all routes south. These defenses were all mutually supporting and reinforced by bunkers, wire, mines, and entrenchments. *Widerstandsnest* 12 and 14 blocked the river road and the path to Colleville-sur-Orne. Built around four R699 casemates, each housing a French 155mm howitzer, WN12, codenamed "Daimler," was a formidable threat that needed suppression. *Widerstandsnest* 14 was also the headquarters of the 736th Regiment's 1st Battalion.

Defensive positions 16, known as "Morris," and 17, nicknamed "Hillman," denied movement on the road complex south of Colleville. Morris had four 100mm guns in casemates, while Hillman was the command post for the 736th Infantry Regiment and designed for all-round defense. Even if a landing was successful on Sword Beach, the British force would need significant reinforcements to reach Caen's outskirts.

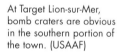

At Target Lion-sur-Mer, bomb craters are obvious in the southern portion of the town. (USAAF)

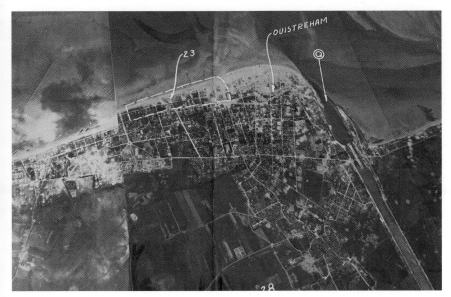

Target 23 was a strong German defensive complex with a unique bunker for employing firing machine guns, a 75mm anti-tank gun in a west-ward-oriented R626 casemate. To the east, on this photograph, the artillery strongpoint shows the effect of the air and sea bombardments. Bomb craters, large and small, are observable across the bottom of the photo. (USAAF)

For the sector that led to Caen, the allocation of bombing targets is perplexing. Capturing the city was Montgomery's most important goal from the beginning of his planning. With it being the hub of the vital rail and road communications throughout the landing area, he intended to reach it on the battle's first day. But given the strength of the German defenses in depth, Montgomery's lack of concentration for his attacking forces and their supporting bombardment is surprising. The planners identified three targets along the invasion beach where the 3rd Division would land. Originally, the plan was to attack the artillery battery in Ouistreham, but the extreme urban nature of the terrain dissuaded them from doing so. However, they labeled Riva Bella (Target 23) as "Ouistreham Battery." Clearly, from the illustrations and coordinates provided by the Eighth Air Force, it was not the main strongpoint the bombers attacked, but the secondary defensive position west of the primary battery.

Utah Beach

The most accurate bombing in Normandy on June 6th took place on Utah Beach, carried out by the Ninth Air Force's IX Bomber Command. Three hundred B-26 medium bombers attacked three groups of German defensive positions along a several-mile stretch of open beach, defended by the 919th Grenadier Regiment, 709th Infantry Division. Here, Lieutenant Arthur Jahnke, a platoon leader in the 3rd Company, commanded *Widerstandsnest 5*.

A little before 0600hrs, Jahnke stood on a sand berm and, looking to the north, saw a wave of twin-engine bombers coming in from the sea. Usually, he watched bombers continue inland, but instead the lead formation of nine aircraft turned left and flew up the beach straight toward his position.

This illustration captures when Jahnke, an experienced and decorated officer, realizes his platoon is the objective for this flight of bombers. They are flying low, and he has just watched as the bomb doors open and 250lb bombs begin tumbling towards his defensive positions. Moments later, he was on the ground as the first wave of aircraft hit his nearby bunkers. The bombs shattered a nearby wagon, and sand and debris almost buried the young officer alive. He managed to find protection from the onslaught behind a concrete wall. He then watched as bombs hit his munitions bunker, causing a massive explosion.

For a moment, he had a chance to evaluate the damage. Everything not protected by concrete was gone. The accurate bombing damaged artillery pieces, buried the rifle pits, and destroyed two munitions bunkers. Bombs hit all of the bunkers but failed to penetrate. His casualties, as a result, were light.

Jahnke and his platoon would do the best they could to defend against the US 8th Infantry Regiment that would land in front of his damaged defenses. Within two hours, overwhelming American power secured the complex, and Jahnke was preparing to board a landing craft on his way to a prisoner of war camp.

Photo array of Ouistreham a week after the invasion. The area with the label "Ouistreham", is the artillery strongpoint and the scene of heavy fighting. Many bomb craters are noticeable in the center of the city, Numbers 27 and 28 are the strongpoints Hillman and Daimler. (USAAF)

Of the coastal targets in the landing zone, BrigGen Frederick W. Castle's 4th Combat Wing had Target 22, WN20 at Colleville. Beginning at 0655hrs, five squadrons of B-17s – each with six aircraft – attacked the German defenders in sequence from an altitude of between 15,000 and 17,000ft. The bombing load consisted of 1,100 100lb bombs and a few 500lb bombs. Castle's 4th Wing also attacked the resistance nest at Lion-sur-Mer, starting at 0655hrs when 37 aircraft arrived at the target, out of an original allocation of 43. This bomb load was exclusively 500lb bombs, some 408 in total.

The attacks against the Ouistreham defenses came exclusively from Jeffery's 100th Bomb Group, part of Col Edgar M. Wittan's 13th Combat Air Wing. Forty-two bombers from this group began taking off around 0200hrs. A little after 0700hrs, they were approaching their targets. From an altitude of 14,000–16,000ft, 41 B-17s – one had to turn back – each dropped 38 100lb bombs. The attack continued for about 20 minutes. This sector of the beach, codenamed "Roger," was the objective for the 1st Special Services Brigade, made famous by bagpiper Private Bill Millen as Lord Lovat's commandos headed off to relieve the defenders at Pegasus Bridge.

The defense at Luc-sur-Mer, which the British in their humor named COD, was the complex defending the Queen Red sector of Sword Beach. The AEAF planners identified it as Target 22, which was the objective for Castle's 4th Combat Wing. Considering it was one of the two primary landing beaches, it received attention from a total of five squadrons from the 94th, 385th, and 447th Bomb Groups. The planners named it as another Ouistreham strongpoint, adding to the confusion as to where the bombs actually fell. Certainly, none of them landed on the German defenders.

The defenses at Lion-Sur-Mer received the codename "TROUT" and were numbered as Target 21. Castle's 45th Combat Wing also had this assignment, and sent seven squadrons from three bomb groups – 42 aircraft in all – against it. Thirty-seven aircraft arrived overhead and dropped 408 500lb bombs on the stretch of coast.

Castle also sent a dozen aircraft to attack Target 27 near Colleville. A 1930 graduate of West Point, Castle was General "Hap" Arnold's godson and one of the first US officers in the United Kingdom after America entered the war. His promotion to wing commander at the age of 36 made him one of the war's youngest general officers, and his post-war career appeared promising. However, he was shot down by German fighters over Belgium on Christmas Eve, 1944. For his bravery in helping most of his crew escape before the airplane crashed, the American government awarded him a posthumous Medal of Honor.

The 1st South Lancaster Regiment and the 2nd East Yorkshire Regiment were the leading elements of Brig Edward Cass's 8th Infantry Brigade. Cass's task was to secure the beachhead at COD and then pass the 185th Brigade forward toward Caen. As the 3rd Division's official history noted: "It seems surprising that General Montgomery had ordered Dempsey… to capture the large, well-defended city of Caen with one infantry brigade." Like the selection of targets, the allocation of forces – just one division – to establish the lodgment, fight through the German defensive positions, and seize the center of the Norman transportation web, Caen, seems haphazard and ill-conceived.

The bombardment did nothing to the Germans other than possibly alert them that an attack was taking place. First on the beach was the 5th Assault Regiment, made up of engineers whose objective was to break through the obstacles and open the way for the infantry. Commanded by Lt Col Arthur Cocks, his engineers, supported by Sherman tanks equipped with flails to beat mines and other sand obstacles, were hit by enemy fire as soon as they landed. The result was that Cocks and 159 of his assigned and attached soldiers perished within minutes, and 15 out of 26 Sherman tanks were destroyed. The plan was for the engineers to open eight lanes across the beach within 30 minutes, but because of the accurate German fire, it took almost an hour and a half to open one lane.

Behind them came the infantry. At COD, the 2nd East Yorkshires suffered about 200 men killed or wounded within a matter of minutes. At TROUT, the 1st South Lancasters stormed ashore and within a few minutes German defenders killed the commanders of both A and B Company. Eleven officers and 126 men of the battalion would not answer roll call the following day. It took until 1030hrs, hours later than planned, for the British to capture the complex. Most of these casualties can be directly attributed to LeMay's bombers not neutralizing the defensive positions as the army planners requested. Certainly, he did not fly his aircraft down the beach as he had bragged at the previous night's meeting. If the bombers had flown down the beach, rather than perpendicular, they would have been much more effective.

This was a dangerous time for civilians. As mentioned earlier, over 100 citizens of Ouistreham perished that day. Many probably died during Bomber Command's assault earlier in the morning, but this later attack contributed to the damage and toll of dead and wounded. Additionally, Luc-sur-Mer, Lion-sur-Mer, Colleville-sur-Orne, and several other villages suffered more than 50 civilian deaths, mainly from the morning's assault. Aerial photographs across the coastline from the period clearly display concentrations of bomb craters away from the landing beaches and, especially in the British and Canadian sectors, within French towns and villages.

Major General Samuel E. Anderson's IX Bomber Command was the principal attacking force in support of the US 4th Division on Utah Beach. It performed brilliantly, the damage it caused to the German defenses ensuring a relatively smooth landing. It was the only air element to accomplish its mission on the morning of June 6. (USAAF)

Ninth Air Force

After arriving in London in January 1944, Eisenhower and Montgomery reviewed COSSAC's original *Overlord* concept. They decided to add another beach to the invasion plan on the Cotentin Peninsula, codenamed "Utah," to expand the landing area and facilitate the American capture of Cherbourg. Major General J. Lawton Collins, the US VII Corps commander, had the task of coordinating both the 4th Infantry Division's amphibious landing and the parachute assaults of the 82nd and 101st Airborne Divisions.

AEAF planners assigned Louis Brereton's Ninth Air Force to neutralize the beach defenses rather than the Eighth's heavy bombers. Whatever the reason for this decision, there were undoubtedly enough heavy bombers available to engage these targets. However, the decision proved wise, as this was the most decisive and accurate action of any bombing mission on the morning of June 6. All of the aircraft – 542 A-20 and B-26 medium bombers – came from Maj Gen Samuel E. Anderson's IX Bomber Command.

Anderson had two tasks that morning. The first was to launch attacks against six artillery batteries: three in the American sector and three in that of the Commonwealth forces. These included batteries in Ouistreham, Pointe du Hoc, and Maisy, which other bombers

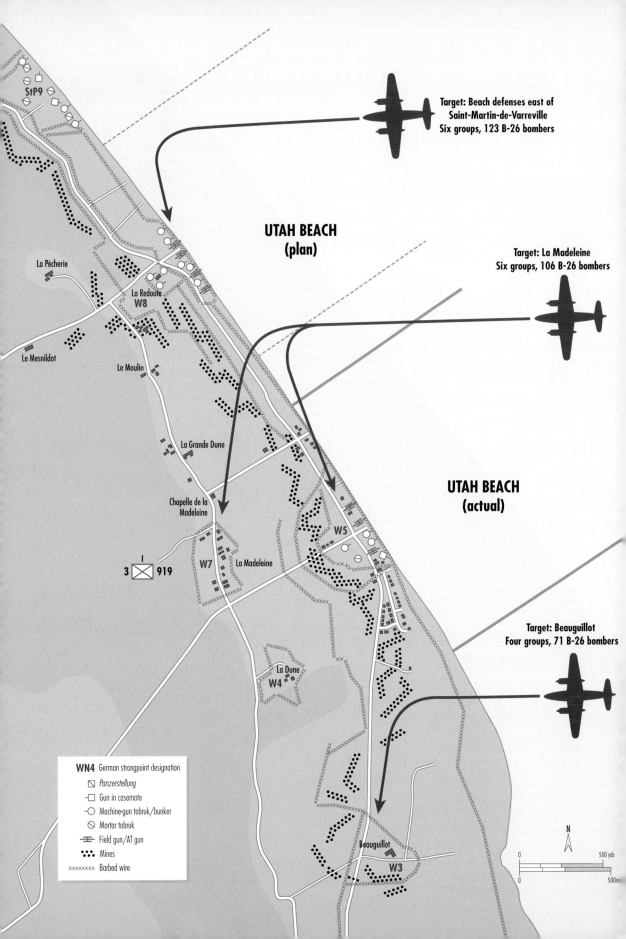

Target: Beach defenses east of
Saint-Martin-de-Varreville
Six groups, 123 B-26 bombers

**UTAH BEACH
(plan)**

Target: La Madeleine
Six groups, 106 B-26 bombers

StP9

La Pécherie

La Redoute
W8

Le Mesnildot

Le Moulin

La Grande Dune

**UTAH BEACH
(actual)**

Chapelle de la
Madeleine

W5

3 ⊠ 919

W7   La Madeleine

Target: Beauguillot
Four groups, 71 B-26 bombers

La Dune
W4

WN4 German strongpoint designation

⟋ *Panzerstellung*

⊟ Gun in casemate

⊸○ Machine-gun tobruk/bunker

⊘ Mortar tobruk

⊧ Field gun/AT gun

• • • Mines

xxxxxxxx Barbed wire

Beauguillot

W3

N

0   500 yds

0   500m

had attacked earlier. Two other targets included a battery in Bénerville-sur-Mer, northeast of Houlgate, and Montfarville, near the tip of the Cotentin Peninsula. His second task, and most important from this book's perspective, was to attack seven German defensive positions along Utah Beach. Again, as with the Eighth Air Force, the purpose was to neutralize these defenses so that the assault teams from the 8th Infantry Regiment, 4th Infantry Division, could secure a beachhead. From there, the division would attack west to link up with the 101st and 82nd Airborne Divisions that parachuted onto the peninsula earlier that morning, and at the same time begin moving north towards Cherbourg. What made this operation different from those of the heavy bombers was that navigators and pilots could often see their targets and make changes in their bombing approach. In addition, they would attack parallel to the shoreline, not perpendicular like the Eighth Air Force. While more dangerous for the crews, it greatly reduced the possibility of hitting American soldiers in their landing craft.

NINTH AIR FORCE FIRST MISSION JUNE 6, 1944						
Time	Description	Type	Aircraft	Bomb Groups	Bomb Size	Tons dropped
0443	Bénerville (Vic Houlgate)	Artillery Battery	2	391st	2,000lb	2
0445	Ouistreham	Artillery Battery	2	322nd	2,000lb & 1,000lb	1.5
0550	Pointe du Hoc	Artillery Battery	17	391st	2,000lb	16
0557	Maisy	Artillery Battery	18	391st	2,000lb	33
0600	Beauguillot (St Marie du Mont)	Coastal Defense	71	323rd, 344th, 387th, 397th	250lb	106.5
0600	La Madeleine (Utah Beach)	Coastal Defense	106	323rd, 344th, 386th, 387th, 394th, 397th	250lb	159
0600	Saint-Martin-de-Varreville	Coastal Defense	123	323rd, 344th, 386th, 387th, 394th, 397th	250lb	184.5
0600	Montfairville (Vic Barfleur)	Artillery Battery	16	322nd	2,000lb	30

Lieutenant Colonel Günther Keil's 929th Grenadier Regiment had responsibility for the coastline where the American 4th Infantry Division intended to land. The seven installations were so close that separating one from another was difficult for navigators then and historians today. Often, the flights attacked the objective to the north or south of the one the planners had assigned them. Therefore, it is best to examine the defenders and attackers according to three main defensive groupings: the complexes at Saint-Martin-de-Varreville in the north, La Madeline in the center, and Beau Guillot on the southern edge.

Saint-Martin-de-Varreville

In the northern portion of this sector, opposite Saint-Martin-de-Varreville, the Germans established three strong defensive positions. In the north at Les Dunes de Varreville, the 4th Company, 199th Regiment, constructed Strongpoint 10, Hameau Mottet. This position blocked the route from the coast to St Martin and then the interior road network. Surrounded by wire, it had a casemate-mounted 75mm gun oriented north on its left flank and two 47mm antitank guns on its right, all protected by concrete casemates. In addition to two Tobruk-mounted tank turrets and a 50mm gun on a ring-stand, it had a host of mortars and machine guns. In the center of this complex, the 3rd Company commanded Strongpoint 9.

Bearing special striped markings on wings and fuselage, a B-26 Marauder of the US Ninth Air Force charges at low altitude over the English Channel on June 6, 1944, to attack gun installations and coastal defenses, while landing craft below head toward the Normandy coast. (Photo12/UIG/Getty Images)

This modern defensive complex contained five tank cupolas mounted in Tobruks, two 88mm antitank guns, machine guns, and a mortar. Concrete bunkers and casemates protected all of these positions. Barbed wire, mines, and a tank ditch added to the installation's all-around protection, while a large searchlight completed the defensive equipment.

The southern portion of the line was WN08, sometimes referred to as La Redoute, also manned by the regiment's 3rd Company. It blocked the road from the beach to the crossroads at d'Audouville la Hubert. Primary armament included a 76mm cannon, two 80mm mortars, two 50 mm cannons, and a 47mm antitank gun. It also had its complement of wire and mines.

La Madeline

In the center of this defensive complex was WN05, commanded by Lieutenant Arthur Jahnke, a platoon leader from the 3rd Company. A young officer recently decorated for service on the Eastern Front, his platoon operated a 75mm gun, two 50mm guns, a 47mm antitank gun, and a Tobruk-mounted machine-gun tank turret. It also had several additional machine guns and a mortar. To the rear was another small command post, WN07, that served as the company command post. Finally, to the south was WN03 in the village of Beauguillot, which could not assist the defenders at WN05. It had only one 75mm gun, a tank turret mounted on a casemate, and a 50mm gun.

Against the three fighting positions near Saint-Martin-de-Varreville, Anderson sent 162 B-26 bombers, with 123 of them making it to the target. The standard bomb load for each aircraft was a dozen 250lb general-purpose bombs. However, with the cloud cover often thick, the planes flew below the planned altitude of 7,000ft, often dropping their ordnance at only 4,000ft. As a result, many pilots reported they missed the target or bombed the wrong one. Some, however, were certain they hit the assigned objectives and put them, at least temporarily, out of business.

The two mutually supporting defensive complexes would be a challenge for the American landing forces under any circumstances. Friction, however, intervened on the side of the American invaders. Guide boats could not lead the first wave to the correct landing, and deposited them 1,500 meters to the south. An infantry-engineer task force, based on the 3rd Battalion, 22nd Infantry, would capture both of these positions from the land side by the end of June 6.

Beauguillot

Anderson sent six groups of 18 aircraft, with 71 of them arriving at the target, to bomb Beauguillot and its nearby defenses. None of the bombardiers believed they were on-target. Still, given the weaknesses of the positions, the "fair" assessment seems to have been enough to keep it from interfering with the American landing further north. Later that morning, the 2nd Battalion, 8th Infantry Regiment, had little problem overrunning the shocked defenders and seizing the southernmost exit off the beach.

The main drama on Utah Beach took place at La Madeline, where the landing vessels mistakenly deposited BrigGen Teddy Roosevelt, Jr, Col James Van Fleet, and the reinforced 8th Infantry Regiment. Generally unsupported by defenders to the north and south, the Germans would face the entire 4th Infantry Division alone. Six groups of 18 bombers each targeted the location, 106 aircraft finding the enemy defensive position and pounding it with 250lb bombs. Because of the cloud cover, the pilots dropped extremely low, bombing at altitudes as low as 3,500ft.

Lieutenant Jahnke survived the war, so we know what happened that morning from his perspective. A little before 0600hrs, he stood on a dune overlooking the English Channel.

His unit had been on alert for several hours and believed their resistance nest was ready. He glanced north and saw a wave of twin-engine bombers flying in from the sea in textbook formation. Normally, Allied bombers continued inland to attack other locations, but not today. He watched as the lead formation of nine aircraft made a left turn and headed down the beach straight toward him. He ducked into a dugout and watched the planes with his binoculars; as the belly doors opened, the bombs tumbled out of the aircraft. He dropped his binoculars and pressed his face into the sand: "Thundering hell. Flashes. Smoke. The reek of explosives." The next group of bombers hit his position directly, and he could hear the whistles as they fell. The explosion rocked him against a wall and tipped over a cart-load of sand on top of him. In pain, he burrowed his way out and jumped into a bomb crater. Then, realizing the aircraft might be dropping antipersonnel bombs, he ran for a concrete wall. Bombs hit his munitions bunker, and he watched as everything inside exploded. Then, when it was quiet, he got up and ran around his position. "Everything they had dug-in in weeks of work had been torn apart as if on a children's playground," he thought. Many of his weapons were knocked out or unserviceable. But he had not lost many soldiers, since most had been in their bunkers during the air assault. Then there was another attack, this time going after his two 50mm cannons. Jahnke thought these aircraft had rockets, but they would not have come from IX Bomber Command. He watched both gun positions blow up, killing most of the crews and destroying the guns.

The IX Bomber Command attack on the Utah Beach defenses was exactly what Collins and Bradley had requested. While the air attack had little effect on the concrete emplacements, it had seriously damaged or destroyed most exposed crew-served weapons. According to a Ninth Air Force study, 300 B-26 Marauders dropped 4,414 bombs on Utah Beach, totaling more than one million pounds of explosives. Fifty-nine percent of those bombs detonated within 500ft of their targets, including 16 percent of strikes that were direct hits, or very nearly so. This accuracy, under difficult conditions, was an exceptional performance.

A few moments after the bombers left, naval guns opened up and continued to keep the German defenders from mounting an effective resistance. Then the infantry landed on the beach, accompanied by Sherman Duplex Drive tanks, which helped the 8th Infantry overcome the remaining defenses. Within an hour, the defenders of WN05, including Arthur Jahnke, were under guard and preparing to move to prisoner camps in England. The 8th Regiment's casualties that morning were incredibly light, with only 29 killed and 110 wounded. The Joint Fire Plan, in this case, worked as designed.

That evening, Maj Gen Raymond O. Barton, commander of the US 4th Infantry Division, and his artillery commander, BrigGen Harold W. Blakeley, felt satisfied with the events of the day. The division had accomplished most of its objectives thanks to the element of surprise, partially caused by landing in the wrong area, and the air and ground bombardment support. It had moved off the beach, linked up with the paratroopers from the 101st Airborne Division, and begun the long fight north to Cherbourg. Casualties were very light; the brutal fighting was ahead of them in the next few days. Since the regimental commanders had events well in hand, and the chief of staff was still getting the headquarters up and running, the two generals had little to do. Deciding it was time to visit their portion of liberated France, they jumped into their M20 Weasel tracked vehicles to inspect the area, it still being light around 2100hrs. They drove up the beach and examined the bunkers demolished by the bombardment. They were especially interested in examining the fortifications opposite their intended landing area at Saint-Martin-de-Varreville, particularly Strongpoints 9 and 10. They were astonished and appreciative of the damage inflicted by the Ninth Air Force and the naval gunners. Unlike the Eighth Air Force's heavy bombers that failed to destroy the German fortifications on Omaha and the other beaches, the medium bombers of the Ninth were precise. Their accurate air attacks had prevented enemy gunners from interfering with the landings and creating needless casualties among the American troops.

ANALYSIS AND CONCLUSION

British troops assemble on Gold Beach and prepare to continue the assault. The bunker in the background was subdued by infantry from a previous wave. (Keystone-France/Gamma-Keystone via Getty Images)

Historians have generally ignored the role of the Allied air forces on June 6, 1944. Besides analyzing the Transportation Plan, the AEAF's program for destroying the rail yards in France and Belgium, there is little discussion of bomber participation in the invasion. For more than 75 years, most of the standard works on the Normandy assault have dismissed the Eighth Air Force's involvement with general comments noting that they overshot their targets. In some cases, historians note that the staff changed the bombing plan to save lives, which General Eisenhower supposedly approved. Meanwhile, aviation historians regale readers with statistics that discuss the grandest bombing raids of the war, such as RAF Bomber Command's assault on Cologne in May 1942, with 1,046 aircraft, the Eighth Air Force's assault on Berlin in March 1945, with 1,221 heavy bombers, or both air forces attacking Dresden in February 1945, with 1,296 aircraft. Yet these raids pale in comparison with the efforts of the US Air Force and RAF on D-Day.

The first combined assault that morning against coastal defenses, with over 2,800 aircraft from Bomber Command and the US Eighth and Ninth Air Forces, was the largest of the war, by any measure. By individual service, Bomber Command's 1,300 aircraft and the Eighth Air Force's 1,350 bombers were their most extensive assaults of the war. This incredible demonstration of Allied bombardment capability did not end with that first wave of aircraft. From the evening of June 5/6 to the following night, more than 5,000 heavy bombers attacked targets in support of the ground forces landing on the Normandy invasion beaches. All day long, thousands of Allied bombers continued to hit towns, bridges, and rail yards across France. For example, at 1330hrs, 56 B-24 bombers from Hodges' 2nd Division arrived over Caen. Without warning, they bombed the center of the city, where citizens were at the market gathering supplies to take to their hiding places. Within a few moments, over 400 of them were dead and another thousand wounded or traumatized. Bombers from the Ninth Air Force returned at 1630hrs, while Bomber Command joined the fray later that night. From Caen alone, there were over 1,741 deaths, thousands more wounded, and still thousands more joining groups of refugees trying to flee to safety. For the next week, Allied bombers would continue to destroy French cities to prevent German troops from using their roads. Why, then, has so little historical attention been focused on this massive aviation effort?

Firstly, the mission was not in line with Harris, Spaatz, and Doolittle's doctrinal focus. US and Royal Air Force historians and publicists have played down their participation in this part of the war. Operating within the theoretical framework created by Douhet, Trenchard, and Mitchell, they sought to take the fight to German industry and the country's population. These heavy bomber commanders seriously believed they could end the war without placing a single Allied soldier in France, other than as a mop-up force after Hitler and his regime surrendered. Supporting the invasion was not a welcome diversion, especially for the American commanders,

General Erwin Rommel and his staff inspect the Atlantic Wall. Especially in the Normandy area, these understrength defenses would have been neutralized and ineffective if hit by heavy bombers. (Bettmann/Getty Images)

who were determined to create an independent airforce after the war. Their participation in the Joint Fire Plan was precisely the kind of role they did not wish to perform: serving as the Army's long-range artillery.

A second reason for not celebrating the airforces' bombing in Normandy is because they killed French citizens, precisely the people the Allies were seeking to liberate. We have already noted that the initial bombardment resulted in the death of hundreds of civilians, the wounding of many others, and the destruction of much of their property. By the end of the day, Allied bombers would kill over 1,300 civilians in the *département* of Calvados, plus another 725 in the Nord in support of *Fortitude*. The physical damage was significant, as the historic centers of places such as Caen, Lisieux, Falaise, St Lô, and Coutances became piles of rubble. Villages such as Norrey-en-Bessen, Aunty-sur-Oden, and Condé-sur-Noireau ceased to exist. By the time of the Allied breakout from Normandy in July, over 8,000 civilians had perished, most of them at the hands of Allied bombers. We should also remember that in most instances, few Germans were present when the bombs tumbled from the sky, since the heavy bombers struck beyond the front lines. It is no wonder the Allied bombing effort in support of Operation *Neptune* has received so little official attention.

In its official assessment, Eighth Air Force deputy operations chief Col Walter Todd noted:

The immediate beach areas showed only limited evidence of bombing damage as was to be expected in view of the extra precautionary measures taken to avoid short bomb falls when the overcast bombing technique was used. [Those precautions included the arbitrary time delays on bomb releases.] Areas behind the beachhead, ranging from 300 to 400 yards to three miles revealed extensive evidence of concentrated bombing patterns. The principal contribution made by this bombing effort was the demoralization of enemy troops and the disruption of signal and transport communications, which hindered the deployment of immediate reserves.

However, despite such comments, this was not the mission; they were supposed to neutralize the beach defenses. The final reason for officially ignoring this massive display of airpower, therefore, is that it generally failed. Only on Utah Beach, where IX Bomber

American B-24 bombers in action over Normandy. Although not taken during the D-Day morning mission, this photograph gives an idea of the aircraft's altitude and method of bombing. These were not precision attacks, and bombs could fall far from the planned target. (Keystone-France/Gamma-Keystone via Getty Images)

Command flew low and delivered its bombs on target, did airpower accomplish the tactical wishes of the ground commanders. In contrast, 1,300 Lancaster and Halifax bombers were incapable of neutralizing ten coastal artillery batteries that morning. Allied warships dueled for much of June 6 with German gun crews that survived the air assault. In the end, it was the firepower from the US and Royal Navies that put these installations out of action. Meanwhile, 1,400 Liberators and Fortresses were incapable of inflicting any damage on 45 defensive positions. Very few Germans perished or suffered wounds under the almost 3,000 tons of bombs the Eighth Air Force deposited along the Normandy beaches – a spectacular indication of failure. And while the bombardment certainly caused many to lapse into shock or become disoriented, sufficient German gunners and infantry handled their weapons, causing needless casualties among the landing forces. Much of the blame for this failure rests with a handful of colonels at Eighth Air Force headquarters. These planners failed to consider in their calculations the infantry commanders' desires and the fate of the soldiers wading ashore. Despite their later arguments, the staff changed the plan, not for operational purposes, but to prevent potential bad publicity. Passing off this change by alleging that the Supreme Commander approved it only accentuates one's disdain for this irresponsible decision.

It is reasonable to consider what other options existed. Using heavy bombers as long-range flying artillery was odious to Harris and Spaatz. Once Eisenhower decided to use this class of aircraft in the invasion, the bomber commanders could have embarked on one of two courses of action. What they did, of course, was attack as ordered and send their aircraft to bomb tactical targets. They employed the same formations and techniques they used when assaulting cities, ports, and factories in the heart of Germany. In western France, the Luftwaffe was ineffective, and few large antiaircraft guns were in place to intercept the bombers. The planners employed none of their creativity to explore other means of accomplishing their missions.

Could they have employed different formations, perhaps smaller ones? Was it possible for the bomb wings to attack from a different perspective, such as along the beaches rather than across them? Could they have integrated fighters into the assault to mark targets and guide the bombers? It is illustrative of the organization that they did not better consider how to support the soldiers in the landing craft. That was their task, and, as far as we can tell, they expended no effort in applying creativity to their assigned roles. To his credit, only Doolittle explored the option of using H2X under these conditions, and prepared his crews to do so. This lack of creativity and adaptation by the bomber commanders in this instance is not unique. It would happen again in other situations, most infamously during Operation *Cobra* in late July, when the bombers flew over the heads of American ground forces rather than parallel to the troops as Bradley requested, killing and wounding many in the process.

The bombardment of France by American and British aircraft is a topic that historians have long ignored. But rather than ending the discussion with the D-Day bombing, it is much better to use it as the place to start an examination of what happened and why.

FURTHER READING

Although the D-Day assault is one of the most examined events in military history, historians have generally ignored the air portion of Operation *Neptune*. This is especially true when considering the Allied air forces' support of the invasion that morning. Books about the Eighth Air Force and RAF Bomber Command concentrate on the physical aspects of missions against German targets, usually ignoring the effects of their raids on objectives in France. Published accounts of the Ninth Air Force provide more details, especially since it was designed to execute these kinds of missions and it performed well that morning. Standard invasion accounts, written from the infantryman's perspective, essentially ignore the air bombardment, except for short remarks that the bombing produced little and contributed to Allied casualties. More promising are the German accounts of the invasion that began appearing at the beginning of this century. French accounts, prepared by local universities in the Normandy area, are most helpful and provide excellent details on what happened and who perished in the air assault.

The most important document to understand the air effort for Operation *Neptune* is the British Air Ministry's three-volume *RAF Narrative (First Draft): The Liberation of North West Europe*. Written from the perspective of Leigh-Mallory's headquarters, it addresses all aspects of the assault, including order of battle, techniques, and the details of all air elements involved. This is the essential reference. Copies are available from the RAF Air Historical Branch (https://www.raf.mod.uk/our-organisation/units/air-historical-branch/second-world-war-campaign-narratives1/).

Government reports and records

In addition to the RAF narrative, other government reports are helpful to organize the details of the air assault. Most of these are available from the Air Force Historical Research Agency at Maxwell Air Force Base (http://airforcehistoryindex.org). Others are available at the UK National Archives; the National Archives and Records Administration at College Park, Maryland; the Ike Skelton Combined Arms Research Library at Fort Leavenworth; and the Eisenhower Presidential Library. In most cases, copies of these documents and reports are located at multiple locations and many are now posted on the internet.

Allied Expeditionary Air Force, *Operation Neptune, Allied Expeditionary Air Force Overall Air Plan*, Dwight David Eisenhower Presidential Library, Abeline, KS (1944).

Allied Expeditionary Air Force, Joint Planning Committee, "AEAF Bombing Operations Committee Meetings May 29–May 31," AIR 37/505, National Archives (UK), Kew, UK (1944).

Allied Expeditionary Air Force, "Minutes of Allied Air Commanders Conferences (May–July)," Air 37/563, National Archives (UK), Kew, UK (1944).

Allied Expeditionary Air Force, "Daily Int/Ops Summary No 131, 6 June 1944," Imperial War Museum, London (1944).

Allied Expeditionary Air Force, "Daily Int/Ops Summary No 133, 7 June 1944," Imperial War Museum, London (1944).

"Commander, SHAEF Neptune: Joint Fire Plan (8 April 1944)," RG 331, Box 66, NARA, College Park, MD (1944).

George, Robert H., *Ninth Air Force, April to November 1944*, Air University, Maxwell AFB, AL (1945).

Headquarters, Eighth Air Force, "Eighth Air Force Tactical Operations in Support of Allied Landings in Normandy, 2 June–17 June 1944" (1944).

Headquarters, Eighth Air Force, "Eighth Air Force History, (June)" (1944).

Headquarters, Eighth Air Force, "Monthly Summary of Operations: June 1944," RG 243, Box 1, NARA, College Park, MD (1945).

Headquarters, Eighth Air Force, "The Role of H2X on D-Day," Stanford University, Hoover Institution Archives, Frederick L. Anderson Papers (1944).

Headquarters, Bomber Command, "Bomber Command Intelligence Narrative of Operations No. 818" (1944).

Headquarters, Bomber Command, "Bomber Command Intelligence Narrative of Operations No. 818, June 6" (1944).

Headquarters, IX Bomber Command, "Mission Summary, Field Order 348-S, 6 June 1944," RG 243, Box 42, NARA, College Park, MD (1945).

Parker, Maj Thomas R., "Statement of Results of D-Day Bombing by 4 Engine Aircraft," Prepared by History Section, 8th Air Force. 8 August 1944, RG 319, Box 1/72, NARA, College Park, MD (1944).

Reference books

Certain reference books are essential for understanding the operations of these airforces. Most useful to this author were the following:

Bowman, Martin W., *USAAF Handbook 1939–1945*, Sutton, Stroud, Gloucestershire (1997).

Falconer, Jonathan, *Bomber Command Handbook: 1939–1945*, Haynes Publishing, Newbury Park, CA (1998).

Freeman, Roger A., *Mighty Eighth War Manual*, Janes, New York, 1984.

Freeman, Roger A., Crouchman, Alan & Maslen, Vic, *Mighty Eighth War Diary*, Arms and Armour Press, London (1990); Chronology, Janes (1981).

Harris, Arthur T., *Despatch on War Operations, 23 February, 1942 to 8th May, 1945*, edited by Sebastian Cox & Hoorst Boog, Frank Cass, London (1995).

Middlebrook, Martin & Everitt, Chris, *The Bomber Command War Diaries: An Operational Reference Book*, Viking, New York (1985).

Official histories

Published official histories often establish the framework for later historical studies. While full of important information, they represent the organization and seek to present it in a positive light. Historians' findings and analysis may be overruled by uniformed officers who either participated in the event or have other agendas. The following have proved very informative:

2nd Information and Historical Service, US Army, *Omaha Beachhead (6 June–13 June 1944)*, American Forces in Action Series, Vol CMH Pub 100-11, Historical Division, War Department, Washington, DC (1945); Official History (1994).

Craven, Wesley Frank, & Cate, James Lea, *Volume Iii: Europe, Argument to V-E Day, January 1944– May 1945*, The Army Air Forces in World War II, University of Chicago Press, Chicago (1951).

Ellis, L. F., *Victory in the West, Vol 1: The Battle of Normandy*, HMSO, London (1962).

Greenhous, Brereton, Harris, Stephen J., Johnston, William C. & Rawling, William G. P., *The Crucible of War, 1939–1945: The Official History of the Royal Canadian Air Force*, Volume III, University of Toronto Press, Toronto (1994).

Ruppenthal, Roland G., *Utah Beach to Cherbourg (6 June–27 June 1944)*, American Forces in Action, Vol CMH 100-11, CMH, Washington (1948); CMH (1984).

Stacey, C. P., *The Victory Campaign: Operations in North-West Europe 1944–1945. Official History of the Canadian Army in the Second World War*, Vol III, Queen's Printer and Controller of Stationary, Ottawa (1960).

German defenders

Historians have paid more attention to the German defenders in the last 20 years. Of varying quality, they give readers an understanding of what the bombardment meant to those in the bunkers.

Bernage, Georges & François, Dominique, *Gold, Juno, Sword*, Heimdal, Bayeux (2003).

Bernage, Georges & François, Dominique, *Omaha Beach*, Heimdal, Bayeux (2015).

Bernage, Georges & François, Dominique, *Ste-Mère-Èglise, Utah Beach, Ste-Marie-Du-Mont*, Éditions Heimdal, Bayeux, France (2014).

Carell, Paul, *Invasion! They're Coming! The German Account of the D-Day Landings and the 80 Days Battle for France* (trans David Johnston), Schiffer Military History, Atglen, PA (1995).

Drew, Richard, "Atlantikwall Co Uk," http://www.atlantikwall.co.uk.

Hargreaves, Richard, *The Germans in Normandy*, Pen & Sword, Barnsley, South Yorkshire, UK (2006).

Severloh, Hein, *WN62: A German Soldier's Memories of the Defense of Omah Beach Normandy, June 6, 1944*, H.E.K. Creativ Verlag, Garbsen, Germany (2016).

Trigg, Jonathan, *D-Day through German Eyes. How the Wehrmacht Lost France*, Amberley Publishing, Gloucestershire, UK (2020).

Zaloga, Steven J., *D-Day Fortifications in Normandy*, Fortress 37, Osprey, Oxford, UK (2005).

Zaloga, Steven J., *The Devil's Garden: Rommel's Desperate Defense of Omaha Beach on D-Day*, Stackpole Books, Mechanicsburg, PA (2013).

Zetterling, Niklas, *Normandy 1944: German Military Organization, Combat Power and Organizational Effectiveness*, Casemate, Philadelphia (2019); J. J. Fedorowicz Publishing (2010).

The French

Often ignored by Anglo-American historians, the French were active participants, as well as victims, during Operation *Neptune*.

Boivin, Michael & Garnier, Bernard, *Les Victimes Civiles De La Manche Dans La Bataille De Normandie: 1er Avril–30 Septembre 1944*, Centre de recherche d'histoire quantitative, Caen (1994).

Boivin, Michael, Bourdin, Gérard & Quellien, Jean, *Villes Normandes Sous Les Bombes (Juin 1944): Les Normands Témoignet*, Presses Universitaires de Caen, Caen (1994).

Passera, Françoise & Quellien, Jean, *Les Civils Dans La Bataille De Normandie*, OREP Éditions, Bayeux (2014).

Quellien, Jean & Garnier, Bernard, *Les Victimes Civiles Du Calvados Dans La Bataille De Normandie: 1er Mars 1944–31 Décembre 1945*, Editions-diffusion du Lys, Caen (1995).

Other secondary sources

Few historical events have more books and articles published about them than the landings on June 6. Those that might help the reader understand the event include the following. This is not an all-inclusive list:

Baldoli, Claudia & Knapp, Andrew, *Forgotten Blitzes: France and Italy under Allied Air Attack, 1940–1945*, Continuum International Publishing Group, New York (2012).

Balkoski, Joseph, *Omaha Beach: D-Day June 6*, Stackpole Books, Mechanicsburg, PA (2004).

Balkoski, Joseph, *Utah Beach: The Amphibious Landing and Airborne Operations on D-Day*, Stackpole Books, Mechanicsburg, PA (2005).

Bourque, Stephen A., *Beyond the Beach: The Allied War against France*, Naval Institute Press, Annapolis (2018).

Bourque, Stephen A., "Operational Fires: Heavy Bombing of Norman Towns on D-Day" In *Canadian Military History* 19, no 2 (Spring) (2010), pp.25–40.

Bourque, Stephen A., "Rouen: La Semaine Rouge," scholarly article in *Journal of Military and Strategic Studies* 14, nos 3 & 4 (2013), pp.1–34 (www.jmss.org).

Caddick-Adams, Peter, *Sand & Steel: The D-Day Invasion and the Liberation of France*, Oxford University Press, Oxford, UK (2019).

Copp, Terry, *Fields of Fire: The Canadians in Normandy*, University of Toronto Press, Toronto (2003).

Darlow, Stephen, *D-Day Bombers: The Veterans' Story: RAF Bomber Command and the US Eighth Air Force Support to the Normandy Invasion 1944*, Grub Street, London (2004); Stackpole Books, Mechaniscburg, PA (2010).

Davis, Richard G., *Carl A. Spaatz and the Air War in Europe*, Center for Air Force History, Washington, DC (1993).

Doolittle, James H. & Glines, Carroll V., *I Could Never Be So Lucky Again: An Autobiography*, Bantam Books, New York (1991).

Ford, Daniel, "The Only Bombers to Hit Their Marks on D-Day," Airspacemag.com (2019), https://www.airspacemag.com/military-aviation/mission-utah-beach-180972310/.94.

Hastings, Max, *Overlord: D-Day and the Battle for Normandy*, Vol. RG 407, WWII Operational Reports, 1941–48, Simon & Schuster, New York (1984).

Hughes, Thomas Alexander, *Overlord: General Pete Quesada and the Triumph of Tactical Air Power in World War II*, The Free Press, New York (1995).

Knapp, Andrew, *Les Français Sous Les Bombes Alliées, 1940–1945*, Tallandier, Paris (2012).

McManus, John C., *The Americans at D-Day: The American Experience at the Normandy Invasion*, Forge Books, New York (2004).

McManus, John C., *The Dead and Those About to Die. D-Day: The Big Red One at Omaha Beach*, NAL Caliber, New York (2014).

Miller, Donald L., *Masters of the Air: America's Bomber Boys Who Fought the Air War against Nazi Germany*, Simon & Schuster, New York (2006).

Orange, Vincent, *Tedder: Quietly in Command*, Frank Cass, London (2004).

Overy, Richard, *The Bombing War: Europe 1939–1945*, Allen Lane (Penguin Books), London (2013).

Saward, Dudley, *Bomber Harris*, Doubleday & Company, Inc, Garden City, NY (1985).

Tedder, Arthur William, *With Prejudice: The War Memoirs of Marshal of the Royal Air Force Lord Tedder, G. C. B.*, Little, Brown and Company, Boston (1966).

Wakelam, Randal T., *The Science of Bombing*, University of Toronto Press, Toronto (2009).

INDEX